Who the Pooh are You?

Celebrating Our Differences

By

Steve Geyer

with Holly Smith

Scriptures taken from multiple translations of the *Bible*.

Edited by Holly Smith

Cover image by Word Alive Publishing

Steve Geyer
https://stevegeyercomedy.com/

Holly Smith
https://hishollysmith.org/

Published by Slow Men Productions

ISBN: Print 978-1-4866-2023-4
ISBN: eBook 978-1-4866-2024-1

Words of Praise for this Work

"Steve's insight into personality-types transformed our marriage and helped us view ourselves and others differently, all while having a good laugh."
Heather & Roger Goldsmith

"Healthy dialogue and understanding have become lost arts. Now more than ever, we need *Who the Pooh Are You?*. You'll laugh, cry... and understand yourself and others like never before! We all know that effective communication is a foundational tool for relationships. I've toured extensively with Steve and have witnessed countless, couples' lives impacted towards deeper, richer relationships. Steve has an uncanny knack of blending humor, psychology, creativity, theology, and story.
Embark on an equipping journey with the Winnie the Pooh characters of your childhood... and rediscover the wonder of life through deeper wells of compassion and joy in your relationships!"
Rob McKinley
Manager, Church Relations
Union Gospel Mission, Vancouver

"Steve Geyer is not only hilarious, but he's incredibly authentic! His use of humour disarms you, and then once you've let your guard down, he presents truth in such an understandable way, you can't help but be changed! This book will help you understand yourself better, and those around you! This message has impacted me in a way I'll never forget" Mark Miller/Billy Graham Association Canada

Table of Contents

Grateful to A. A. Milne for Creating Characters That We Can All Relate to…

Foreword: In Which We Begin with a Bit of Thanks and Explanation

The vast majority of the existing published materials and educational resources on personalities are *incredibly helpful*, so THIS book would not exist without the ground-breaking work and research that great minds, researchers and other authors did. The reason that I decided to write this book was certainly not because I wanted to—I had absolutely no desire to add one more project to already overrun bookshelves on personalities—unless, of course, there was a really good or even a moderately good reason for it. People from all across the US and Canada have been encouraging me ***for years*** to write this down, because it *helped them so much*, so I took this as a justifiable reason to put a verbal presentation that I've been doing for nearly twenty years onto paper.

But first I had to get over the notion that, "if I thought of this... it can't be very good." I ultimately and begrudgingly had to admit to myself that some of the insights and take-aways about personalities that I accumulated over the years were fun and kind of clever ways of helping people (especially in marriages) deal with some tough interpersonal issues, however I thought they were for "in the moment" and I didn't think they would necessarily be long-lasting. But after touring a comedy show for couples for the last ten years--doing several hundred shows and receiving a few thousand emails--apparently, I was wrong. Not only was what I shared during these comedy shows helpful in the moment (the night of the show), but weeks, months and even years thereafter. And then came the emails and the requests for a book... the ***very book*** you're holding in your hands.

Steve's thanks: There are always more people whose names should appear in this part of any book; so, if I missed you, please forgive me and know that you are more than welcome to write your name in this section.

My family deserves most of the credit for this book, as they were unwitting participants when I first started this over twenty years ago. I'm grateful for the pioneers who first discovered the core attributes of different personalities and subsequent deeper understanding.

Here are a few names, in no particular order, that deserve to be recognized for their part of this project coming to fruition: Roger and Heather Goldsmith, Jordan and Danielle Raycroft, Robert McKinley, Mark Miller, Steve and Brooke Lensink, Eric and Marcia Spath.

If not for Holly Smith conspiring with my lovely wife, you would not be reading this book at all. Holly's superpower is encouragement and knowing what I'm trying to say and putting it into a readable format.

Thank you, Ken and Carolyn Drez, for believing the best in me and loving me like a son. I love you as if we shared the same last name.

Thank you, Kathy Geyer, for never giving up on me, even when I gave up on myself.

Thank you, Kirsten Butler and Graham Geyer, for being the best daughter and son a dad could ask for.

Lastly, thank you, Lord, for creating us from our fingerprints all the way down to our personalities so that we may take hold of that for which Christ Jesus took hold of us to fulfill our destinies.

I (Holly) would like to especially thank my Chris for all of his love for me—*always letting me dance* (as our friend, Phillip Sandifer, once wrote). It's been a running principle that has made our marriage such a blessing, full of space to fly and to flail and especially to love one another more deeply every day—always with Jesus, showing us the better way. I could not have done this without him! I would like to thank my mom, Elizabeth Gorin, whose artistic gift has always astounded me. What a gift *she* is! I also would like to thank Steve for entrusting me with his heart-work here. It is a joy and honor to serve with him! Anything I have added has been such a blessing to bring to others. Thanks to my wonderful children Noah, Kylie, Tabor and Sydney, who have prayed for me and brought laughter, brain breaks, some coffee, conversation and much joy my way. I would like to thank my friend Bev, who infuses me with messages of encouragement on days fraught with darkness. She has always brought me Jesus' light and His Word. Finally, I give all my heart-filled thanks to my Savior, Jesus, who has not only brought me thus far, He also came with me, continually blowing a fresh wind of grace, insight and encouragement to take each step with boldness and faith.

Dedication

To Kathy Geyer, my all-time favorite Rabbit.

For: Harrison Jude Geyer and Jameson Beck Geyer... and for any future grandchildren yet to come.

In Which There Must Be an Introduction

"The things that make me different are the things that make me ME."

A.A. Milne

After years of spending lots of time, money and other resources on an individual quest (I was going to say ***journey***, but the word ***quest*** sounded more epic and adventurous) to better understand my personality and so become a better me—while at the same time trying to figure out other people, so that I might *play better with others*—I discovered that there's a seemingly endless supply of books, materials and resources written on the subject. Most of these approaches were quite helpful, and some were (*quite*) not. Since what I do for a living (comedy) is observing and then commenting on the human condition, neither the helpful nor the non-helpful resources were ultimately a waste of my time, as I learned from both.

So, with a seemingly endless supply of books, materials and other resources already written on the subject of personalities... why write another one?

I'm so glad you asked! ... or that you read the question that I just asked (*wink*).

Since I'm not a psychologist, psychiatrist or any other "ist" of record (*well, maybe a humorist!*), I wanted to make this fun, easy to learn and easy to remember ("sticky") —so then, I definitely needed to make these personalities more lovable! *But how?* Hmm... I'll find something that is widely recognizable and universally beloved. I got it!

Who else, but a "silly old bear?"

With greatest respect to A.A. Milne, we (Holly and I) wanted to represent the characters of an owl, tiger (With an extra *g*), piglet, rabbit, bear and donkey graphically to help you understand the *Who of You* in this story. However, we found that there are no substitutes for the beloved characters.

This resource is intended to be educational—a fun and easy way to learn about yourself and the people in your life, helping you understand why you do the things you do, like the things you like and why you don't like certain things...and certain people.

But you may ask, *another book on personality-types?* Yes and no. There are already a vast number of books and resources available on personality-types. Some books are great some are okay, and some are well... you decide.

So why bother writing another one? I'm glad you asked! But before I answer… let me ask you a question to ponder… since there are so many already… why write another love song?

Our purpose for this book is to explain personality-types in a way that is fun and easy to remember with the goal of improving interpersonal relationships. It's not intended to make you an overnight expert on personality-types or to become better at business. That said, if and when you put some of what you learn from this silly old book, you will probably become better in business, but you'll never be an expert on personality-types…no one is.

Like other books on this topic, there are some generalities that will be used to present and explain each personality. And because ***we are all unique and not fashioned by a cookie cutter***, there are complexities and nuances from all four personalities that make your core personality trait unique as well.

This book is less technical in its approach and more relatable and relational. The use of Pooh characters should have been the first clue. But this book is for you and your families to explore better ways to not only know yourselves better, but to appreciate the differences of others better, sprinkled with some humor, which makes every family a little bit better together, I think.

It is important to note, to pay attention to, to give credence to, to be mindful of this fact—not everyone in your family will have the same or even similar personalities. You and everyone you are related to are unique and different even though you draw from the same DNA and gene pools.

At its core, this book is written with the hope that you will be able to make the connection to the spiritual aspect of personality-types... *you know... the God part, as well.* For I believe God is the very Source of it all—of *us all.* And He doesn't work haphazardly.

Connecting to the Source: Shaped by God's Hand

If we can embrace the notion that we were *uniquely* created by a Creator for an intended reason and purpose, it is easier to accept and embrace our particular personality-type rather than trying to deny it, mask it (pretend to be somebody else) or run away (hide) from it. It also helps us to accept and embrace other people's personality-types and not run away from them either.

"For we are his workmanship, created in Christ Jesus for good works, which God prepared beforehand that we would walk in them" (**Ephesians 2:10 BLB).**

If you are a Christian, you probably have that verse on a refrigerator magnet or know someone who does. It's a fairly straight-forward verse and doesn't require a lot of explanation… *or does it*? Basically, that verse states that everyone has a destiny or purpose—that we're supposed to be here. But wait… there's more to it.

Let's look at that verse again with some of the words enhanced in my paraphrase: *"For **we are** God's workmanship, created in Christ Jesus to do good works in which He has prepared in advance for **us** to do."* **Ephesians 2:10***

Take another look, there appears to be a general exhortation. Since the author of Ephesians, the apostle Paul, under the inspiration of the Holy Spirit starts the verse with *we* and ends with *us*, I've heard this verse taught as a *collective body of Christ* verse rather than a verse about individuals <u>within</u> the body of Christ. In other words, focusing on the *we* and *us*, many pastors have encouraged their congregations to adopt a personality or trait for which the church will be recognized in their local community. And this is a good thing! However, not everyone in the church may have the innate personality-type to effortlessly achieve the church's mission statement. What pastors would do well to remember is that their personality-type influences their way of seeing God's purpose for the congregation they serve. Here's another way to read the same verse.

*"For **I am** God's workmanship, created in Christ Jesus to do good works in which He has prepared in advance for **me** to do."* **Ephesians 2:10**

I know that I changed some of the words, but not the meaning or intent of the scripture. The verse still says the same thing, but it's more personal now. Paul did not intend for this verse to be read only as a collective, but also as individuals; so that ultimately, the collective could work. When Paul uses *we* and *us,* he is including himself. In other words, he's an individual part of the whole. We are also individual parts of the whole. We matter; we belong; and we're supposed to be here. Let's look at the same verse again, but now with different emphasis.

"For we are God's ***workmanship,*** *created in Christ Jesus* ***to do good*** *works in which He has* ***prepared in advance*** *for us* ***to do.****"* **Ephesians 2:10**

Because Jesus was a carpenter by trade, it seems only natural that we'd picture a piece of wooden (or perhaps stone) furniture as our mental image example for workmanship. If we lived during that period of time that would make a lot of sense. But the workmanship takes on a whole new meaning in the 21st century.

When Paul chose this word, it meant more than just the finished project. It includes all that went into creating the finished project: first came the creative thought process and then deciding on what to use for the project. What is the ultimate purpose of the finished project? Who will use it? Is it for indoor or outdoor use? What type of wood is best? And so on...

There were no milling machines, no electric hand tools and certainly no video tutorials from which to watch and learn. First century tools consisted of axes, chisels, mallets (hammers), adze, hand saws and tools for sharpening. Carpentry was an exhausting vocation that required a lot of physical strength, time and skill.

And because there were no machines, each piece of furniture or workmanship was unique. A carpenter could make four chairs to be in the same set, but they were all, in some ways, different. They are all chairs—and they look the same—but they were individually created by hand; therefore, they are not exactly the same. *Are you starting to see the point I'm trying to make?*

Ephesians 2:10 is the foundation upon which *Who the Pooh are You?* is written. **It's my belief that our personalities are God-given and not a result of our environments, experiences, birth order, family systems or even our traumas.** If we are, in fact, the workmanship that Paul speaks of, everything about us is intentional—from our physical attributes to our personality-type. I think it would be rather cruel of God to create us with a personality-type that does not align with the good works He prepared in advance for us to do.

Do environments, experiences, birth order, family systems and trauma influence or have an impact upon us and our personality? *Absolutely!* They can certainly affect our personality for both good and bad. *But our core personality still remains.*

Gondola Stop #1

Let me introduce you to a vehicle to better drive an understanding of **your very important place in the Bigger Story's timeline** (the Bigger Story is God's own timeline). It's a gondola used not to travel across the water, but one that goes through the air. A gondola is an enclosed cabin on a ski lift that carries passengers on a thick cable up and down a mountain. So, hop in the gondola with me (Holly) to get a better perspective at the bigger picture of why celebrating our differences really matters for the long haul.

When I (Holly) was a young married, I took a summer vacation with my Chris' parents to New Mexico. We went to Taos and Angel Fire. It was gorgeous from the ground, as we drove around, but nothing *NOTHING* compared to our ride on the gondola. From the gondola, you could see *for miles*. My perspective shifted, as the view became unhindered. The mountains were no longer in the way of my vision for I had a grander spot from which to see. It is like that and more, when you consider the view God has from **His very own timeline**. *We are all a bunch of short lines beneath it.* And He cares about those lines—and us.

In fact, He created them and us for a larger purpose. So, picture with me that timeline for a minute from our gondola vantage point today. Just what might God be doing on the larger scale with all of our current day-to-day issues? It is certainly something worth considering.

With that consideration in mind, also ask God this one burning question: ***What is <u>my place</u> in Your Bigger Story?*** And as Steve pointed out, it says in the *Bible* that we are God's workmanship (His masterpieces, His poems, His greatest works!) created in Christ Jesus to *do good works*, which He planned in advance for us to do. (Ephesians 2:10) Adding that piece of the puzzle to the question above is quite wondrous, really. You see, God planned in advance good works for you (His masterpiece) to do on His Bigger Story's timeline...good works that matter. And, in fact, YOU matter. *<u>You</u> are the wonder.*

Are you trying to know yourself and others better? In other words, are you on a quest, like me?

Well then, let's ride together!

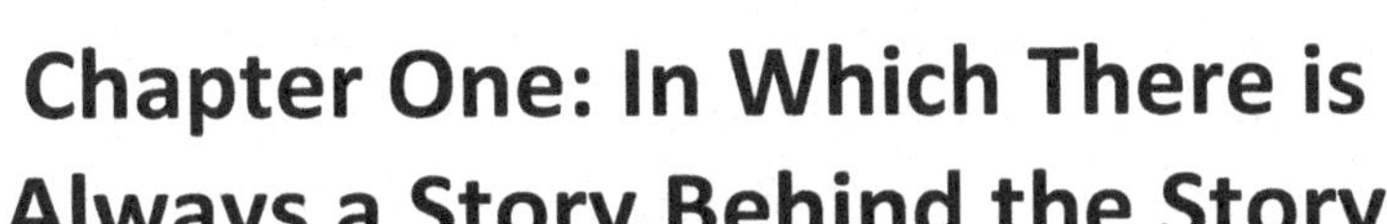

Chapter One: In Which There is Always a Story Behind the Story

"When you are a Bear of Very Little Brain, and you Think of Things, you find sometimes that a Thing which seemed very Thingish inside you is quite different when it gets out into the open and has other people looking at it."

A.A. Milne, Winnie-the-Pooh

Have you ever wondered why you do the things the way you do? Or why the way other people do things drives you crazy? Would the world be a better place if other people (especially the people in your daily life) would just do what you deem as *normal behavior*? At one time or another, we have probably all had these thoughts.

One of the greatest things we could ever give ourselves is the gift of healthy *self-awareness*. Self-awareness is defined as, *"a conscious knowledge of one's own character, feelings, motives and desires."* *

For more than twenty years, I have utilized many well-known personality profiles to help people uncover things about themselves and discover things about others.

Whether in counseling or leadership training sessions, using personality profiles is extremely helpful, because they enlighten and empower people toward personal growth. People learn the why's of what they and others do, which most often leads to better interpersonal relationships. Unexpectedly, after using these personality profiles, I came to realize that there are two common results -- and it took quite a while for me to even notice!

The first thing I discovered is that more often than not, it is difficult for people to remember which word, letter, number, color or animal is associated with which personality-type they are—especially if there are combinations of numbers or letters. Unless people had it written on a card that they kept in their wallet or on a chart taped to their refrigerator, people spent a lot of time going back through a list to match themselves to their corresponding personality-type; and usually by then the conflict at hand is escalated even further. So, I wondered, *how could I make these personalities easier to remember?*

Secondly, there was a tendency for a person to give themselves a *free pass* for their personality, and then use another's personality as a bludgeon or an indictment against them. It was not uncommon to have a couple in my office in the throes of an argument and one of them categorically and defensively state, *"Well that's just the way I am!"* and in the very next breath look at me while employing a dismissive tone and say about their spouse, *"Well you know how their type is..."* How could I make these personalities more endearing—especially to each other?

Who the Pooh are You? was created to allow people to see themselves *and others* in a non-threatening and very often endearing light. It helps people to accept their own personality-type, using beloved characters, while viewing others in the same way. Instead of referencing a letter or numeral to describe yourself or another person, when someone is referred to as *Tigger*, it often deescalates a dispute.

Using real life stories and scenarios, ***Who the Pooh are You?*** teaches couples that their partner or spouse may not be purposely trying to irritate them. What one partner perceives as an intent to provoke or frustrate them is merely just Piglet being Piglet and Owl being Owl. *Of course, Tigger being Tigger may be on purpose.*

Also, parents and children benefit from a quick and simple method of learning about each character, so it is easy to retain the information. And it helps parents to identify traits in their children early, as well as helping older children learn how to better communicate with their parents and siblings.

Introducing the Four

Each character is unique while at the same time having similar or crossover thoughts, attitudes and behaviors to the other characters… which explains why certain characters get along and why some characters don't.

There are inherent strengths (or gifts) associated with each of the four characters. Some things "just come naturally" to them. Most of us have no problem believing that some people are just "born" with musical or athletic talent. I lived in Nashville, Tennessee for many years, so a lot of my friends happened to be musicians and vocalists. They are incredible; but whenever I complement them on their talent, most of them would react almost in embarrassment and reply, "Aw thanks, I was just born with it."

Some were born into families of musicians, so they were exposed to music very early and grew up in a musical environment. It makes sense that they would know how to play an instrument or read music… but you can't learn how to have a voice like Michael Bublé… you either have it or you don't.

Other friends were born into families with no history of musical talent; and yet, seemingly, from out of nowhere… they just had a "knack" for music or a voice that angels envy. Most of the musicians I know work hard to improve or refine their gifts, but I have to tell you that

I know a rare few that are (irritatingly) amazing without much effort. Keep in mind that for most of us mere mortals, natural talent only gets a person so far.

Likewise, we can be born into a family of academics and score 1600 on the SAT and be the only kid in the family that struggles with geometry.

Similarly, personalities are not something that are inherited. Obviously, certain traits, behaviors and values are taught and reinforced in families. But having a bad temper, being judgmental, selfish or lying are not specific to a certain personality-type. *Each character has a propensity toward sin because that is just human nature.* So, having a bad temper is only a family trait if we choose to inherit it.

So, you might be an Owl born into a parliament of Owls and the nest is orderly and tidy, but you could also be a Tigger that shakes up the family tree. You might be just another Rabbit in the litter and everyone *EVERYONE* knows exactly what they want, or you could be the lone Piglet still trying to decide if you even like corn.

Here is a quick look at what some of each character is *born with* or naturally gifted toward.

OWL
Order
Organization
Information or data
Clarity
Identifying problems

RABBIT
Control
Leadership
Solutions to problems
Direction
Answers

PIGLET
Harmony
Understanding
Compassion with action
Deference
Hospitality

TIGGER
Acceptance
Fun
Ideas
Excitement
Spontaneity

Included in each of the four character/personality chapters to come, you will discover that they skip along the following garden path:

1. First, they explain a specific character.
2. Next, there will be examples and insights given that are common to the other characters, as well.
3. Then, as we learn about a particular character, the other three characters are in the mix, as a way of highlighting what they all have in common and how the different characters respond in certain situations or how they interact with one another.
4. In following this path of understanding ourselves and others, it is vital that we accept that no character is better or worse than the other. Each character is equally important and equally valuable. To believe otherwise will hinder your ability to accept yourself and extend the same courtesy to those around you.

It is not lost on me (being a comedian) how humorously ironic it is that so many of the insights into understanding myself and others came from a fictional character, who is described as having **"a head stuffed with fluff."* And in all candor... some of the people that I've paid good money to for counsel and advice could be described in the very same way.

If there is an actual goal in publishing this, it's to help you become comfortable *in your own skin*, while not letting others get under it. It's to give voice to your feelings and to answer the why's and reasons for our actions and behaviors. It's what a bear with "a head stuffed with fluff" knows. Hopefully, you'll know as well soon enough.

How this all came to be (a Backstory if you will)

Years ago, when I first began leading short-term humanitarian relief trips to poor communities in the US and abroad, I discovered that although all the volunteers had a common purpose to serve the needy, they behaved and expressed themselves in different ways. This difference caused more than a few unexpected conflicts, and even altercations, between a bunch of really great people, who were all wanting to help the needy. Trying to get a group of volunteers—who varied in age, were from different backgrounds and came from different cities—to work as a team in difficult and often stressful situations became quite a chore. Two of the kindest and most generous people I'd ever met would be at each other's throats over doing a good work. After a couple of trips, I thought that it might be helpful to use personality profiles as part of pre-trip training, so everyone could better understand themselves as well as everyone else on the trips.

Being a fan of personality profiles, I knew of several resources that I could use. After narrowing it down to three books on personalities (See Appendix B), I realized that I still needed a quicker, simpler and more fun way to teach personalities. Using some of the insights from various resources, I broke down the four basic personalities from a *different point of view*. I added stories and scenarios that I had experienced or encountered, as well as some stories that others had shared with me.

But I still needed to explain each personality in the following ways:

1) Each personality would be easy to recognize.
2) People identified with and understood that personality.
3) People felt compassionate towards that personality.
4) People could retain the information and remember that personality.

Using numbers, a letter, color or even an animal had already been done--and sometimes people had trouble remembering which numbers, letter, color or animal was which personality. Knowing that, I was racking my brain and trying to figure out what to do, so a coworker who was sitting in my office made a suggestion.

If you came into my office, you wouldn't have to be a rocket scientist to figure out that I am a huge fan of Walt Disney. The wall art, my desk set, the countless number of Disney® figurines (not to mention my Mickey Mouse®

watch) would be kind of a clue. *"Why don't you use Disney® characters?"* my coworker asked. Sounded good to me, but after running Mickey, Minnie, Donald, Daisy, Goofy and Pluto through my mind, I didn't see that any one character had any particular personality trait that stood out from the others. *By the way, Donald could use some help with anger management.* After mulling over several more Disney® characters my coworker picked up the little plastic Piglet that sat on my desk and asked, "What about Pooh?"

I knew instantly that this was the answer that I was looking for! All four characters and the personalities they represented hit me at once. I knew that the four would be Owl, Piglet, Rabbit and Tigger and ***Who the Pooh are You?*** became a part of my next pre-field orientation training... and every pre-training since.

Teenagers and adults alike took to it like a duck to water. *After just the first session, where I gave a simple overview and couple of examples for each character, volunteers were speaking to one another using the names of the characters. Team members were laughing, as they identified each other during the break as Owl, Piglet, Rabbit or Tigger.* Spouses were identifying one another, siblings were, too. My favorite part was listening to parents and their kids identifying themselves and each other. It worked! And to tell you the truth, I was actually shocked at how much fun they were having—and even more how quickly they grasped it. My next shock came six months later.

A couple who had been on one of these trips asked to meet with me for some marriage counseling. After they came into my office and we exchanged pleasantries, I asked them why they wanted to see me. Without hesitation Emily said, "You know Rob's a Rabbit, and he's driving me crazy!" Well, knock me over with a feather. It had been at least six months since the trip and probably seven months since pre-field orientation; and yet Emily used "Rabbit" to describe Rob. Not only did she *get it*, but she also retained it. I disguised my shock and proceeded to use the language of "Who the Pooh are you?" while discussing their issue. Rob joined right in stating that Emily's Owl side was driving him crazy.

Soon after my meeting with Emily and Rob—and a few tweaks to focus on *relationships* rather than just *team building*—***Who the Pooh are You?*** became an intricate part of my pre-marital counseling work. In fact, the very first thing a couple did was to take a test that I created to discover which character they were (see Appendix A: print out and take the test yourself!). After working with many couples, I found that even after many years they still use ***Who the Pooh are You?*** to communicate their needs to each other.

In 2007 I was invited to perform at a new, live event called *Couples Night Out*. After a few years and nearly

100 shows, I introduced a 15-minute version of ***Who the Pooh are You?*** to the show. It was a hit! Now after 7 years and over 300 shows across the US & Canada, ***Who the Pooh are You?*** is a 45-minute presentation that closes the show each night. Like those pre-field orientation sessions after the show, couples leave arm-in-arm affectionally referring to each other as Owl, Piglet, Rabbit or Tigger.

So, let's take a leisurely stroll to the 100 Acre Wood and discover, ***Who the Pooh are You?*** *shall we?*

Chapter Two: In Which We Begin to Discover the Who of Pooh

"A day without a friend is like a pot without a single drop of honey left inside."

A.A. Milne, Winnie-the-Pooh

It's okay to be you. I know that sounds like I'm pandering, but I want you to keep reading. You see... personality-type will determine who even picks this book up in the first place.

Some will become engrossed in this book and intently read it cover to cover and back again.

Some will read it with a pen in hand correcting grammarical mistakes (by the way that word should have been grammatical), become frustrated with run on sentence structures and a host of any number of other miscues.

Others, if they even open it, may scoff at the content, will skip around and read it intermittently... in the bathroom or only if someone thrusts it into their hands while insisting, "You have to at least read this one chapter!!"

And lastly there are some who will try to read it and after turning a few pages will realize that they have no idea or memory of what they just read.

So, I get it. I understand.

Understanding ourselves is the only way that we can begin to understand others. So again… **It's okay to be you.** It may or may not surprise you, but a lot of people have a hard time liking themselves.

Most of us grew up learning and can even quote **The Golden Rule** –
"Do unto others as you would have them do unto you."

The Golden Rule only works when we utilize what I like to call **The Platinum Rule** -- "Love others as you love yourself."

Sadly, even after many centuries, humans still have a hard time putting these two simple rules into practice… especially the second one.

Love yourself? What? How dare anyone love themselves! That's just wrong! In our modern or popular culture, when someone is considered as "loving themselves," they are often labeled as being narcissistic. Granted, narcissists do exist, but they are not as common as you might think. You may not have ever met a clinically-diagnosed narcissist (less than 10% of total U.S.

population). If you have, I'll bet that they didn't actually love themselves. Because of name-calling and armchair psychiatry on social media, when people came to me for counseling, many displayed revulsion when I would ask if they loved themselves.

One of my favorite quotes of all time is a prayer from St. Francis of Assisi:

"O Divine Master,
grant that I may not so much seek to be consoled, as to console;
to be understood, as to understand;
to be loved, as to love.
For it is in giving that we receive.
It is in pardoning that we are pardoned,
and it is in dying that we are born to Eternal Life.
Amen."

That's amazing right? Well, I took another look at it and had a thought that I hope our beloved St. Francis would be okay with. You see the part where he says, "to be understood (**by others)**, as to understand **(others)**" (emphasis mine). My hope is that St. Francis might be okay with the notion that in our efforts in seeking to understand (others), we can begin by first seeking to be understood (by ourselves). And that's not to be confused with requiring or insisting upon understanding from others, as we seek self-understanding, but in order to export something to others freely—with no strings attached.

Isn't it only sensible and right to own it first?

Birth Order and Family Systems

May I suggest that you are the way you are for a variety of reasons? I concede that there are a lot of contributing factors to why people think the way they do and do the things they do, but there is still a fundamental factor that people dismiss and often misuse in conversation—but it's true. Simply put, "You and I were born this way".

After years of study and research, I've discovered that gender has absolutely nothing to do with personality-types. There is no such thing as a gender-specific Rabbit or Piglet. Some have tried to characterize Rabbit as masculine and Piglet as feminine and nothing could be further from the truth. I've also come to realize that birth order, family environment and life experiences can have positive and negative effects on your personality, but--for lack of a better phrase--your personality is hard-wired.

Identical twins share the same DNA, eye color, skin tone and facial features. Even though they grew up in the same family environment, they share the same birth order and most likely share a lot of the same life experiences in their formative years. They each have distinct and unique personality traits. They each have a preference for different music, foods and fashion. They are identical in almost every way, except for their personalities. Interesting, one twin may have the same personality-type as another sibling who is not their identical twin.

Birth order and family environments *DO* have an influence and impact on our personality. Starting with birth order, it's important to realize that our family environment had more to do with where our parents were emotionally, mentally and even financially when we arrived than it had to do with us. If they were young, immature and in debt, does it stand to reason that they may have been a little tense and overly stressed and relied on daycare or babysitters more than when the youngest sibling arrived?

Gondola Stop #2

Hop back on the gondola with me (Holly), as we look at the Bigger Story's timeline again. Picture with me a very large building....so huge that it can be clearly seen from the sky for miles and miles and miles away. Now picture that building, figuratively. The Bible says that we are the temple of God, as believers in Jesus Christ. We house the Holy Spirit of God—He is in us all. I know it can be overwhelming to imagine the awesomeness of such a concept. But keep looking at the large building that is far off. That building is a picture of the Body of Christ—all believers in Christ make up that **one building**.

Not only that, but we each have something that we are to accomplish with other believers and with Christ as the Cornerstone of the giant building. This is the why of the who of Pooh. Not for narcissistic value, to stare at ourselves and become so enamored by our beauty (though we are in fact God's beautiful works of art), no—we are looking at who we are and who others are, so that we may operate more fluidly, as one, for a greater purpose. On the Bigger Story's timeline, our purpose is to carry out God's good plan on this earth—and that plan, in tandem with Jesus, as our Cornerstone, is to bring others into the Bigger Story to come along with us, too. *But more on that later...*

Two by fours

Every time I (Steve) have ever built anything there's always at least one 2x4 involved. Your house and my house are full of them. I'd wager that in a garage, shed, pick-up truck or somewhere else you've got one or at least pieces of one tucked away.

Because I like to keep things simple and to help people get the most out of this book, it's built on two by fours.

- There are four core personality-types, four core needs and other groupings of fours.

- There are also twos. There are two core ways of processing, two core ways of dealing with people and other groupings of twos.

These two by fours are the foundational elements for discovering your and other people's personality-type. By using this simple 2x4 method, it will build or create a solid or memorable foundation for each of the personality-types, their core need, the way they process information and the way they are with others. As you read further and travel deeper into the 100 acre wood, these two by fours will serve as anchors or stabilizers, as new information is revealed.

More about the Four Main Characters

If you've ever taken a personality profile test, then I'm sure it's no surprise that I'm going to introduce at least four characters to illustrate four main personality-types. There are many excellent resources available on discovering your personality-type, and these will be listed near the back of this book (Appendix B). Personality profiles typically have a minimum of four and go as high as sixteen different types. I've done my best not to simply rehash the great work of other authors, but to simplify and introduce some thoughts and insights that are significant to each personality. The goal is to help the reader grasp and retain the concept in a fun and endearing way. Because of the Walt Disney Company, A.A. Milne's characters from his classic ***Winnie the Pooh*** tales have been indelibly etched into our collective consciousness.

When disclosing the characters by name, you will most likely already have a certain opinion of them, even before describing the personality of each character. Why? Because of your own personality, your experience with the four characters from books, movies or television affects the way you perceive each character's actions and motives.

Right or wrong, your favorite Winnie the Pooh character may be another person's least favorite and vice versa. As you continue to read further along in the book, the hope is that not only do you visualize these characters and see them with your *mind's eye*, but you will also see yourself and others as these lovable characters, too. Let's meet our four main, lovable—and certainly very recognizable— characters.

"Where's Pooh?" you might ask.

Pooh would be a balanced and healthy combination of **all four main characters**. Why Pooh? Well, as we all know, everybody loves Winnie the Pooh.

"What about Eeyore?" *Ahem*... how do I say this gently... Eeyore is more of a condition than a personality. Eeyore would best be associated with depression or gloominess and since everyone is prone to occasional depression or gloominess, we'll leave Eeyore to the professionals.

Not only does each character represent a personality-type, but they also reveal a core need that is unique to each character. It's important to note that this core need is expressed in a variety of ways, and it is also revealing in the way these characters interact—uniquely—with the other characters.

To gain understanding of a personality that is not your own will take some time, patience and a "look for the positive" approach. Different does not equal wrong. Once you understand your own personality, you'll discover why you struggle with certain personalities more than others.

For instance, Tiggers and Owls often butt heads, while Piglets and Owls rarely do.

Since some characters will skip the Forward and Introduction (*Hi Tigger*), I want to stress that interwoven within each of the next four chapters describing each of the four characters will be stories, examples and insights to help the reader understand each character in certain circumstances or in particular situations.

This is not a textbook; this is not a self-help book… *heck, this was never even intended to be a book*. It's just a way of shining a different light from a different angle on the things that make us unique and different from others. This book is simply the result of wanting to use humor and an old-school-bedside-manner approach to help people accept themselves and the people that they live life with.

Depending on circumstances and situations some characters may be hard to identify because of their unexpected behavior… but that's another chapter.

Come, let's meet Owl.

Chapter Three: In Which Owl Thinks About Everything Logically

"The third-rate mind is only happy
when it is thinking with the majority.
A second-rate mind is only happy
when it is thinking with the minority.
A first-rate mind is only happy when it is thinking."

A.A. Milne

Owls offer order to a chaotic world. Owls are exceptional at adhering to the rules and doing the right thing, the right way and for all the right reasons. Owls are great to have as lab partners in school; because not only have they completed the reading assignment, but they've also already resourced other writings, as well. They always seem to know exactly where their books and other stuff are... because they always put them exactly where they're supposed to be.

Owls live by lists, strive toward accomplishments and absolutely love closure. If you're an Owl even taking the time to read this book is on your list of things to do. Lists help Owl stay on task, know what's left to do and record what they've accomplished so far. I have a friend who is an Owl and when they are having a bad day, they will write something on their "to do list" that they've already done just so that they have something that they could "check off" their list.

Uncompleted projects or tasks that go unfinished can drive Owl up a tree. Owl loves closure because that's just one more thing they can check off their list. During the live version of ***Who the Pooh are You?*** (WTPAY), I repeatedly start a task that I never fully accomplish. Near the end of the show, I ask the audience how many people noticed what I was doing, and if it was "bugging" them. Without exception, each night several people in the audience raise their hands in response. I simply reply, "Hello Owl, it's nice to meet you." The entire audience laughs either at themselves or the Owl they came with, because Owl needs closure. (*You Owls want to know what the task is don't you? Then come to the live show, and you'll see.*)

Owls have the innate ability to discover hidden problems or potential roadblocks while working on projects. They are very punctual, if not 10 minutes early to every meeting or gathering. They are typically very good with finances and can often tell you which store, or which brand, gives you the most value for your money.

Owls love to plan; in fact, it's not uncommon that the favorite part of a vacation for Owl is the planning. Researching the best travel deals, organizing the itinerary and prioritizing what sites should be visited over others are second nature to an Owl. The only thing they don't like about vacation is when family members want to change the plan.

If you are an Owl, your personality is fairly complicated. A lot of people will misread your intent or your actions. Your core need is for there to be **order in your life** (and sometimes that means that order is an expectation put upon others to adhere to, as well). You are an "everything in its place and a place for everything" type. Owls want to know, "Who (*Whoo!*), What, Where and When"... and on occasion, "Why."

Most of the time Owls want the facts without additional commentary. Think of two sportscasters calling a game. One just states the action of the game or the Play-by-Play announcer. The other announcer in the broadcast booth is called the Color Commentator. The play-by-play person just states the facts, while the color commentator weaves tales of the athletes' favorite ice cream flavor and what happened to them in the third grade. Owls are more interested in the box score, statistics and final outcome of the game, while others may prefer to know if there's any more to the story from the third grade. As I stated before, occasionally Owls will want to know the "why," but only occasionally.

We'll get to that.

To understand Owl, you need to know that in their quest to have an **orderly life** and **environment**, they view and approach life uniquely from the other three characters. They process similarly to one of the other characters, but very differently from the other two.

Here's an Owl Overview:

- Desires an orderly life and environment
- Processes using systems and logic
- Thinks and decides analytically
- Follows the rules
- Seeks conflict
- Believes that they're right
- Me-oriented
- Details = Security

At first glance, it might appear that Owls are rather unpleasant people especially in dealing with other people, but once you understand "why" Owls do what they do and think how they think, you'll find that they're much more endearing than you once believed. In fact, it's good to have several Owls as friends.

An orderly life and environment are vital for an Owl to feel secure. They need to know where the checkbook is (and if its balanced), if all the bills are paid and if the dishes are washed, dried and put away (where they're supposed to be) before they can go to bed. Their closets are nearly always organized. They are sorted by colors or groupings such as short or long sleeve, winter or summer and their shoes are paired and precisely perched on shoe racks or lined up neatly on the floor. They are typically creatures of habit and have routines that they rarely deviate from. You can depend on Owl to be prompt, if not early. Owl often tends to give unsolicited advice or opinions, and Owls are usually best-suited for being great physicians, accountants, air traffic controllers and computer programmers. In these vocations, Owl gets you out of the hospital, keeps you out of prison, helps you avoid a premature reservation in the cemetery and makes your computer do what it's supposed to do.

While seeking order in their lives, Owls' thought process goes like this:

"1-2-3-4-5-6-7-8..."

"A-B-C-D-E-F-G..."

"I before E except after C..."

"All my T's are crossed and every I is dotted."

"1-2-3-4-5-6-7-8"

"A-B-C-D-E-F-G..."

(Notice that **emotion** is not part of their process.)

Removing the "3" or the "C " from their sequential order would greatly unsettle Owl. As a result, the removal or interruption of sequential order will result in Owl focusing on the missing number or letter and ignore all the other numbers and letters that remain. "Where's the 3?"... "Where's the C?" they will hoot, as others might not have even noticed the gaps and just leapt from "2 to 4" and "B to D" without even batting an eye. However, Owls don't make that jump instinctively and will be delayed in their decision process until the "3" or the "C" reappears... or in one of those occasional situations I mentioned earlier, need to know "why."

As Owl remains focused on the missing pieces, if there are others that are participating in the decision-making process, they may unintentionally exacerbate the situation by chiding Owl or dismissing him as being "anal retentive," "picky," "difficult" or having "OCD" (obsessive compulsive disorder). Owl is simply trying to process a decision the way Owl is hard-wired or prone to do. Because of a lack of understanding from others on the team, Owl can become defensive—thereby further exacerbating the situation.

Since Owl processes systematically, utilizing logic rather than their "gut" or instinct, the "3" and the "C" are far and away more important to them than the "3" and the "C" might be for others on the team. Notice that I used the word "important" rather than "vital." The missing components are in fact not vital... but to an Owl... **they**

sure seem to be. In situations like this, if someone simply explains to Owl "why" the "3" or "C" is missing it will help Owl to step over a gap that felt more like a chasm.

"Hey Owl, I know the 3 and the C are important, but the 3 and C were lost at sea (no rhyme intended), and we'll never be able to recover them from the depths of the ocean. We have to proceed with the decision process without them, so let's move onto 4 and D now."

This is an occasion when the "why" or the commentary is helpful for Owl, but don't be fooled... they don't want to hear <u>any more than what is needed</u> to proceed, so that great story from the third grade is best saved for another day.

Thinking and deciding analytically makes Owl slow in making decisions. Before Owl makes a purchase, he will do research on the item, which includes reading all the reviews, seeking out the best price, and when applicable, its resale value. After doing the initial research, they tend to research and research and research some more. Even after purchasing the item, Owls will continue researching to make sure they got the best deal.

A simple way to understand Owl's thinking while making a decision is this:

"Ready... aim... aim... aim... aim..."

Decision Making

OWL
"Ready...
aim...
aim...
keep aiming..."

RABBIT
"Ready-
fire-
aim!"

PIGLET
"Okay...just put the gun down."

TIGGER
"We have a gun? Can I see it?"

Rabbits are just the opposite, but we'll get to Rabbit soon enough.

Owl is one who insists upon following the rules. And not only does Owl follow the rules, Owl expects **everyone else** to follow the rules as well. Owl has a tendency to become a self-appointed "referee" in everyday life situations. You can be fairly certain that the person behind you in the "10 items or less" lane at the grocery is an Owl if they tap you on the shoulder and say, "Did you know that you have eleven items in your cart? Yeah... I counted. Those two milks are not considered 'one item' they are two separate milks... you should move over to the next lane...you're welcome!"

You might be laughing or cringing right now, because we have all encountered an Owl. Why? Because most of us have broken the rules. An Owl will even correct another Owl, if the second Owl is unaware of a particular rule. The funny, and sometimes irritating, part is the "You're welcome!" after Owl sends us off to another lane. Why is that?

I'm glad you asked.

Because Owls value following the rules, they inherently believe that everyone else does, too. In fact, they often believe that the corrected party is actually quite grateful for the public correction. Owl is not being a jerk or confrontational for confrontation's sake, Owl just wants to maintain an orderly environment by ensuring that everyone is adhering to the rules. So, an Owl "seeking conflict" often has little to do with the person involved, but the rule that was violated. Unfortunately, it may feel very personal when Owl figuratively throws a flag or blows the whistle. That is unless (of course) if you live or work with an Owl. In those situations and circumstances, if and when you have a history of violating Owl's rules, it can and often will become very personal.

One thing about Owl that is often maddening to the other characters is that they believe that they are **always**

right... about everything. Not only will an Owl restate or inform others of the rules they will also confidently state information as fact. Why? Why does Owl believe they are right? Because they usually are... darn it! Remember, Owls have done the research (and then more research), so when an Owl states something as fact... just go with it.

Owls love lists. They live life by their lists. Nothing gives an Owl more pleasure than to check something off their "to do list." As I said before, I've known an Owl or two who were having a tough day and added to their "to do list" something they recently accomplished just so that they can check it off their list! Lists are how they get through their day and how they can sleep at night. Owls like closure, so when things are left undone or not completed, Owls have a hard time resting... unless they're still doing the research.

Owls are planners, and they stick to the plan. When going on vacation, the greatest joy for an Owl is planning it. They love researching the different activities, the best deals and putting together the vacation itinerary. You know you're an Owl (or married to one) if your family vacation to Walt Disney World® has an itinerary. It probably looks something like this...

Owl's Itinerary *for*

Walt Disney World

Family Trip

8:00 am	Wake up
8:00-8:42 am	Showers
8:45 am	In the Hotel Lobby *for* the "Free" Continental Breakfast
9:05 am	Board the Shuttle to The Magic Kingdom
9:35 am - 3:30 pm	Fun
3:45 pm	Board Shuttle Back to Hotel
4:10 pm	Naps
5:30 pm	Snacks Brought *from* Home
5:50 pm	Board Shuttle to EPCOT
6:30 pm	Dinner in China
7:45 - 10:30 pm	More Fun
10:45 pm	Board Shuttle Back to Hotel
11:30 pm	Brush Teeth
11:37 pm	Everyone in Bed

Repeat Daily

God forbid that anyone in the family starts having fun before 9:35am or that the shuttle leaves earlier or later than expected, because Owl might start fussing and fretting—the times and schedule will be skewed for the rest of the day and will never get back on track. And if you've ever been to Walt Disney World®, you know darn good and well that your wait times are not predictable (and to that end, I recommend downloading the My Disney Experience® app and getting a FastPass® or two).

Because Owl has done the research and created an itinerary, any change to the itinerary creates stress for him and thereby stresses EVERYONE else. To state it plainly, Owls do not like (or more to the point, hate) an unexpected or unforeseen change of plans... and God forbid while waiting in line, Space Mountain® breaks down. That's when the "me-oriented" part of Owl is revealed. But before making a negative assessment and coming to a wrong conclusion about Owl, let me explain what I mean by "me-oriented."

For Owl to be "me-oriented" is not necessarily equated to being self-centered or selfish. Why does a sudden change of plans cause Owl stress and even pain? Because someone just removed the "3" and the "C" and didn't tell Owl that it was coming. Remember how Owl processes, "Ready... aim... aim... aim..."

Additionally, another's desire to change the plans can unintentionally hurt Owl's feelings and send the message to Owl that all his hard work in planning the vacation is not appreciated by the others. This can lead Owls to internalize negative thoughts about the very people he made the plans for. While the one making changes really enjoys the planning process, as well, the original itinerary was created more for Owl's enjoyment than for the others' enjoyment.

It's not that Owl is intentionally trying to be difficult, it's just that a change of plans negatively affects an Owl more than the other three characters. Some characters are indifferent to a change and others love a change of plans. If it took Owl a lot of time to create the itinerary, it will now take time for him to adjust to it. Again, this is how Owls process any decision, unless they are doing simple arithmetic. Owls need to figure out how this minor change might impact the overall itinerary and that takes... you guessed it... time! Given time and the information needed, Owl will eventually come to a decision, but if you're looking for Owl to decide quickly... you might want to go ride Pirates of the Caribbean® (if it's working) and maybe by the time you get back, Owl may be closing in on his final decision.

Here's a work scenario that may shed further light on how Owl processes.

If my explanation of Owl fits someone you work with, try this little experiment.

It starts by not telling Owl that the entire office staff is taking another staff member out to lunch to celebrate her birthday. As everyone is leaving the office for the restaurant, enter Owl's office and slap the birthday card (that everyone else has already signed) on their desk and say, "Quick, sign this! We're all taking Meredith out to lunch for her birthday!" Now stand back and watch the fun, as Owl tries to process what just happened and how it affects their well-planned daily schedule. If you're not an Owl, it may seem odd that your coworker is sitting there stunned with a look of disbelief or confusion. You may even be wondering if you just caused them to have an aneurysm. Nope. Owl is just going through a process.

You see, Owl already had lunch plans and his lunch is currently sitting inside the break room refrigerator—in separate plastic containers that are labeled and dated with their name on each container and note that says, "Do not touch!" because the rest of the staff is not known for following the break room refrigerator rules and etiquette. Add to that, everyone else on staff has had time to sign the birthday card. Owl needs time to decide not only what they are going to write, but where exactly on the card is the best place for them to write it. Will their food in the refrigerator keep for another day? Is Owl expected drive to the restaurant? Will others chip in for fuel? What time will we return to the office? Who's Meredith?

Now just imagine that all of that is going on inside of Owl's head, while someone stands at his desk pushing them to "just sign the darn card" with a look on their face that says, "What is wrong with you?" Owl has enough pressure trying to process, without others negatively assessing or misjudging why Owl has some difficulty making a quick decision concerning a change of plans. It's just Owl being Owl. It's not personal; it's not because they lack intelligence (quite the contrary) or that they don't like Meredith, he just needs time to think through and adjust his plans for lunch and how it might affect the rest of his day. So, when there's a change of plans, consider that Owl is not necessarily being self-centered, inflexible or selfish, but that being "me-oriented" is better understood as him processing "how the change affects me or my previous plans."

In love and life, Owl (like the other three characters) has a choice to make--to be a healthy or an unhealthy version of themselves. It's okay for an Owl to desire an orderly life and environment... that's the way Owl is wired, but... you knew there was a but... when Owl desires order, exactness or perfection more than healthy relationships with others, Owl becomes unhealthy in his quest for order and actually creates disorder in his interpersonal relationships. When Owl's need for order trumps relationships, this is an indication that there is something deeper going on inside of him and has less to do with the change of plans and more to do with some unfinished business inside of Owl's heart and soul.

When Owl can't let the dishes sit in the sink to go play catch with his child... if Owl can't overlook that his spouse has left the twist-tie off the bread (again) or he immediately pulls out the vacuum cleaner when a visiting friend tracks a bit of dirt into their foyer... those are the warning signs of an unhealthy Owl. Order and predictability become more important to Owl than the people they love and care about. If these scenarios feel painfully familiar to you, there's still hope. There's most likely a reason (or several reasons) why Owl has exchanged order for relationships.

As stated earlier in this chapter, healthy Owls make for great physicians, accountants, air traffic controllers and computer programmers. But an unhealthy Owl, one who prefers order over relationships, is often prone to become what others have observed to be Obsessive Compulsive.

We will learn more about Owl in future chapters, like the following:

- Owls desire for justice
- How Owl relates to the other characters
- Why or when Owl began to desire order over relationships
- What happens, if during childhood, Owl is misunderstood or dismissed

So, for now just remember the best way to communicate with Owl is to have "the five w's" (who-what-where-when-and sometimes why) readily available.

Owl Overview

Desires: Orderly life and environment
Processes: Using systems and logic
Conduct: Rule Follower
Decides: Analytically
Life Situations: Seeks conflict
In Conflict: Believes they're right
Interpersonally: Me-oriented
Bottom Line: Details are security

Gondola Stop #3

I (Holly) like to think about Heaven. I'm a dreamer, so as we ride the gondola this time, looking out over the horizon, I want to explore a little bit more of the Bigger Story with you. If you read through the Scriptures, there are so many places, where Heaven (*a real place*!) is described in some detail. Those details for a dreamer like me are stunning to imagine!

Isaiah in the Throne Room of God, saying, "Here am I; Lord, send me!" Then there is John the disciple on the Isle of Patmos with a Revelation-ary vision of King Jesus and His Kingdom that is coming soon. Between these two events in the Bible, I like to picture a man, who was chosen by Jesus to follow Him. He is distraught and has gone off alone—for Thomas (who gets a bad rap for being doubtful) is trying to add up all that Jesus said...and it doesn't make sense.

It is not adding up for Thomas, because Thomas, the disciple of Jesus, is missing some information. He is a literal thinker—like when he heard that Lazarus was dead and he said, "Let's go so we can die, too." But Lazarus would be raised to life from the dead before Thomas' very eyes! Also, Thomas works in exact wording and placement, so when Jesus said, "You know the way to the place I'm going. Thomas replied, "Lord, we don't know where you are going, so how can we know the way?" And of course, Jesus would reply in truth to Thomas that "I am the way and the truth and the life. No one comes to the Father, except through Me." I'm sure

Thomas thought, *what does that even mean?* He might have even believed Jesus was being vague or poetic...certainly not logical to his understanding—not yet anyway!

After Jesus died on the cross, Thomas finds himself alone. When Mary Magdalene and all ten of the other disciples (for Judas had already hung himself) saw the risen and resurrected Lord Jesus, Thomas was not there.

The disciples found Thomas and said, "We have seen the Lord!" Thomas responded, "Unless I see the nail marks in his hands and put my finger where the nails were, and put my hand into his side, I will not believe." *It would be a whole week later* when Jesus would show Thomas his proof. Thomas did doubt; yes, but he doubted because he needed facts and information to confirm the truth.

You see, Thomas is an Owl. And we need Owls in this connected body of Christ. Owls keep us honest. And the Lord? He loves Owls, too. Jesus did not begrudge showing Thomas, but He did remind Thomas that faith without seeing is even better; in fact, those who believed without seeing Jesus would be blessed. I believe that from that moment on, Thomas grew in his faith, adapting to the new information he learned—probably even remembering all the times Jesus had been crystal clear, and he saw it looking back. God is gentle with us, always leading and inviting us further down the road of faith.

Questions for Owls:

1. Does it irritate you beyond simple annoyance when a stranger breaks a rule?
2. Do you find yourself regularly rearranging things "back to normal" around your house or workspace?
3. Do you expect others do things the same way you do?
4. Do you assume that your way of doing things is the only way?

Action for Owls:

1. Extend grace and mercy when others don't meet your expectations
2. Lead with encouragement before bringing a criticism.
3. Though your advice may be correct, try to wait until it's requested before offering it.

By the way, you will notice a common pattern with **all** of the four characters. Because each character has a different core need and values different things, each one is prone to mistakenly believe that others need what they need and value what they value… and that is not the case!

Let’s meet Piglet!

Chapter Four: In Which Piglet Finds His Voice

"I'm not lost for I know where I am. But however, where I am may be lost."

A.A. Milne

An article published by the *New York Times* on February 11, 1990 estimated that approximately 96% of Americans demonstrate Piglet behavior. To clarify, the New York Times didn't refer to the 96% as *Piglets*, that's just what I call them, and that just so happens to be our next character and personality-type.

Like Owl, Piglet is also a very complicated personality... and just so you'll know... so are the remaining two characters. Where Owl is born with a need for order, Piglet is born with a need for a harmonious life and environment. Piglet desires peace, love and on occasion a little Rock & Roll.

For each of our four characters, their environment and family dynamics during childhood will have an impact on their ability to understand and obtain their core need in a healthy way. In other words, they will either be "shaped or warped" by it. To paraphrase a very wise king,

"Encourage your child in what they find interesting, what they are good at, what they enjoy, what they lean or bend toward and when they are older, they will look back to see they have lived a consistent life." **

Family dynamics, environment and life experiences from childhood create variables that shape how we develop our unique way of pursuing and meeting our core need. It's important to note that these variables will serve to shape (*or warp*) the way we behave in meeting our needs, but will rarely, if ever, change our core need. Simply put, we were born this way. Owl will always want order and Tigger will always want... *oh wait...* I'm getting ahead of myself.

So... let's meet Piglet.

To understand Piglet, you need to know that Piglet is a peaceful creature who seeks to live the "life of least resistance" and is the person who is always making sure that everyone else is safe. Ensuring that no one is being left out and that everyone gets a trophy. While all the other children are running to the family car yelling, *"Shotgun!"* Piglet is yelling, *"I want to sit in the middle of the back seat with my feet on the hump!"* Piglet wants everyone to get along and be nice to each other.

Here's a Piglet Overview:

- Desires a harmonious life and environment
- Processes using feelings
- Thinks and decides emotionally
- Bends the rules
- Avoids conflict
- May be right, but doesn't want to hurt anyone else, who thinks that they're right
- Others-oriented
- Harmony = Safety

At first glance you might think that Piglets are pleasant when dealing with other people, and they appear to be rather wishy-washy and weak. But you'd only be partly correct in that assessment. Piglets are typically pleasant when dealing with others, but not always for the sole purpose of being pleasant. Piglet does have a tendency toward being wishy-washy. However, Piglet is not weak, in fact, far from it. Piglets typically have a very high emotional IQ. They are usually thoughtful, insightful, feel deeply and are deep thinkers. When you are hurting, Piglet would be your preferred choice of company over any of the other characters.

Unlike Owls, who need to see all of the research and documentation before seeing the big picture, Piglets have the ability to accurately surmise the big picture before seeing any of the research. They have what I like to call, a well-developed "knower gene," as they instinctively come to correct conclusion—while Owls are still running the numbers.

The harmonious life and environment that Piglet desires is one where there is no conflict, no arguing, no raised voices and everyone's favorite song is *Kumbaya*. Piglet is not one to bungee jump or parachute and routinely discourages others from doing so, as well. Piglet is not a creature of habit like Owl, but has other tendencies that are very consistent, yet hard to spot. Piglet is like a duck on water. Seemingly without any effort, above the surface a duck gracefully glides across the water, but underneath... that duck is paddling its little, webbed feet off! *Welcome to Piglet's world.* By keeping the peace in his life and environment may appear on the surface that he is amiable and easy going, but under the surface he has a tendency to become an emotional and relational "Roadrunner." Piglet works tirelessly to accommodate as many people as he can.

Piglets are like that guy that used to try to keep all the plates spinning on the "Ed Sullivan Show." *Yes, I am that old.* Stay with me, here.

While attempting to keep the peace and all things harmonious in real life situations, Piglet's thought processes may go something like this:

Is Maureen mad because of something I did?
Where's Bill? He seems sad lately, I need to cheer him up.

Mark didn't finish his report, so I'll just go do it, so our boss won't get mad.
I really don't want to eat fast-food, but everyone does so I will too.
That person is making me extremely uncomfortable, but I don't want to hurt their feelings.
As long as everyone else is okay, I'm okay.

Notice that emotion is nearly 100% of their process, and that's what I refer to as their "feeler gene." This "feeler gene" takes precedence, so that all decisions are now going through this feeler. Piglets have a propensity to emotionally spiral downward when there's conflict or when negative feelings and emotions are expressed. Piglet's internal conversations sound like this:

What did I do?
How can I fix it?
Oh, dear oh dear, what to do, what to do?!

In contrast, here's how an Owl would most likely process these same scenarios:

What's Maureen's deal, geez!
Where's Bill? He's supposed to be in this meeting.
They need to fire Mark.
Raise your cholesterol if you want, but I'm not eating fast-food.
Hey, you need to back off.
This is not okay; the sign says ***no fishing****.*

Where Owls focus on facts, Piglets focus on feelings. So, when Piglet is processing something, his feelings (*as well as the feelings of others*) are involved in making a decision. And because Piglets are others-oriented, they tend to measure the feelings of others as having more weight or value than their own. Before Piglet goes to sleep at night, he needs to know that everyone is safe and sound all snug in their beds, all the doors and windows are locked, that no one is angry with each other and especially that no one is angry or disappointed with them. Oh... and if there is an argument about the dishes being left in the sink, he washes them... even though it is someone else's turn to do so.

As you can imagine the amount of emotional energy exerted by Piglets can be exhausting. So, like that duck on the water, gliding across the pond that emotional energy requires an enormous amount of strength. It takes a lot to keep all those plates spinning and from falling on the floor.

Piglets like order but are not readily known for adhering to a ridged routine. Piglet goes along with the flow that is created by the other people in his life. Piglet wants and intends to be prompt, out of respect for the person they're going to meet but is often late because the person he is currently meeting with needs Piglet to stick around for a few more minutes. This scenario creates what Piglet tries to avoid at all costs--conflict. Conflict makes Piglet extremely uncomfortable, because while being genuinely concerned with the feelings of the person he's with, he is as equally concerned with the feelings of the person waiting for him to show up. Piglet's decision to stay a little longer is not analytical, it is emotional. This highly-developed emotional IQ and genuine care and interest in others makes Piglet an amazing care giver, teacher, social worker and counselor. Piglet has an innate ability to empathize with others, who are in distress or in crisis, by extending care and comfort.

Because Piglet doesn't want anyone to be sad or unhappy, he has a reputation for bending (*while not breaking*) the rules. Not for his own benefit, mind you, but for everyone else who is playing the game. He views rules as what keeps everybody safe and makes the game fair. If anyone is not safe or feels like the game is unfair, Piglet will bend the rules to fit the circumstance, so everyone has fun and everyone is a winner. You can "take it to the bank" that it was a group of Piglets who came up with "participation" ribbons and trophies. Piglet would not be the best choice when hiring a new Commissioner for the NFL, MLB, NBA or NHL.

As mentioned earlier, Piglet seeks to avoid conflict at all costs. He has a hard time saying the word, "No." In an upcoming chapter we'll discover that Tigger has the same difficulty, but for very different reasons. Owl has no problem saying, "No!" In fact, *he rather enjoys it*.

Let me explain. If you were to ask Owl to borrow his car, the conversation may be over before you know it.

You: Hey Owl... can I borrow your car?
Owl: No.
An awkward silence ensues...
You: So we're done here?
Owl: Yes.

Remember that this is not necessarily Owl being selfish... if you want to borrow Owl's car you need to give him advance notice... *way* in advance.

Now if you were to ask Piglet to borrow his car, the conversation would go more like this.

You: Hey Piglet... can I borrow your car?
Piglet: Well... I'd really rather that you not.
You: Why not?
Piglet: Well... the last time you borrowed my car, you wrecked it. And when I went to the body shop to pick it up, I discovered that you also used all the fuel so that I ran out of gas and had to walk two miles to a gas station to get enough gas to get me back to the gas station so I could fill up the tank and get to work this morning.
An awkward silence ensues...
Piglet: Here are the keys. (Handing them over)

Owl responds to the request based on an analysis of how it might inconvenience him, and he also remembered that you were the one who wrecked Piglet's car last month. Owl is not going to hand over his car keys to someone he finds irresponsible. Piglet responds to the request based on feelings. Piglet doesn't want to lend you his car; but he also doesn't want you to feel bad for wrecking his car last month—or to feel bad that by borrowing the car it causes an inconvenience for Piglet. After work, Owl drives his car home, while Piglet is still trying to get his courage up enough to ask the person who borrowed his car to give them a ride home... *with his own car.*

Okay, I grant you that may seem to be an exaggerated version of how Owl and Piglet respond to a request, but I can assure you that these scenarios are based upon real people, in real situations and these were their real responses. In 14 years doing pre-marital and marriage counseling, I've seen a lot.

Conflict, no matter how minor, has the potential to tie a Piglet up in emotional knots. If you ask a Piglet what he wants for dinner he will most likely respond with, *"Oh I don't care"* or *"It doesn't matter to me"* or *"Whatever you or everyone wants is fine with me."* In truth, Piglet does have a preference, but you have to guess it. Piglet wants to make sure that his choice or preference is okay with everyone else. At a restaurant he is usually the last one to order and will ask everyone at the table what they are having, as well as asking his server what her favorite dish is, before settling on his choice.

Scott and Heather came to my office one day. Because Heather was a "card-carrying" Piglet, Scott assumed that there was something wrong with her. He believed that Heather was intentionally being difficult. He felt like she wasn't honest with him and very coy. Scott never knew what Heather wanted because when he asked for her opinion or preference, she was so vague, ambiguous and indecisive, that Heather appeared weak to him. Conversations with her had become downright frustrating.

Here's a typical conversation between them:
Scott: Hey babe, you want to go out for dinner tonight?
Heather: Sure, that'd be great!
Scott: Where do you want to go?
Heather: I don't care, you pick.
Scott: Well... how about Sonny's?
Heather: Nah.
Scott: Then how about Marco's?
Heather: Um... nah.
Scott (with irritation in his voice): Then how about The Steak House?
Heather: Why are you getting mad?
Scott (with teeth clenched): I thought you didn't care where we go!
Heather (now about to cry): Why are you always so mean?
Scott (raising his voice): Why can't you ever make a decision?!
Heather (full on tears): I knew this was going to happen!

Scott: UGH!
Heather: UGH!

Did any of their conversation sound familiar to you? Since that New York Times' article did report that 96% of Americans display some forms of Piglet behaviors, let's just assume that their conversation was very familiar to you. As you read their dialogue, which person did you empathize with? Which one made you want to cry... which one made you want to cuss? I guess you figured out that Heather is a Piglet. We'll explore Scott's personality (Rabbit) in the next chapter.

Scott wants to take Heather out for dinner. Heather wants to go out to dinner with Scott. So why did Scott end up at a fast-food drive through eating in the car, while Heather ate a salad at home alone that night? You might get tired of hearing this, but it's because Piglet was being Piglet and Rabbit was being Rabbit. In Scott's mind, asking Heather if she wanted to go out to dinner was an easy question, even for a Piglet to answer! Scott was hungry, even though he loves being with Heather—there was nothing in their pantry or refrigerator that he was interested in eating. So, he went out.

Scott correctly surmised that Heather was also hungry. She too loves being with Scott and the pantry and refrigerator offerings *were slim*. Scott is "three for three" in his summation; so, he asks if she would like to "go out for dinner" and is pleased with her answer. Since Scott was batting 1000, he decided to ask another question, that in his mind, was as easy to answer as his first. But since Scott is not a Piglet, he has absolutely no idea what's going on inside of Heather's heart and mind.

For Piglets to make a choice (that involves or impacts other people) it takes a fair bit of time, and it takes even longer for an unhealthy Piglet to decide. Because of Piglets' natural tendency to prefer and defer to others, when they are tasked with choosing a restaurant, it creates a conundrum because Piglets don't know what everyone else's favorite restaurant is. Piglets have their favorite(s) but want to make sure that it's okay with everyone else. So that's why, when asked to choose, Piglets will defer to everyone else.

So, what does a healthy Piglet's response sound like?
"I'd like to try the new barbecue place on Main Street."
Simple, direct and without qualification or apology, so everyone else says, "Let's eat!"

Now what would an unhealthy response sound like?
"Well... if you really want me to choose, I guess I'd kind of like to try the new barbecue place on Main Street, unless nobody else wants to go there, which is fine with me... because I really don't know why I even suggested barbecue, since you guys may not even like it."
Ambiguous, meandering and apologetic, so everyone else says, *"Are we going out to eat or what?!"*

I asked Scott to try doing something different the next time he wanted to take Heather out for dinner. I asked him to offer her choices, so that she would not be overwhelmed with having to come up with a restaurant out of thin air. I asked him to consider all the restaurants that he knew she liked and then ask, *"Hey Heather, I want to take you out for dinner tonight, I'm thinking Maggiano's, Outback or China Palace? Which restaurant would you prefer or is there another one that I'm missing?"* This made the decision-making process a lot easier for her, because it was now more conversational than just informational. Instead of Scott asking about going out to dinner—because his brain received information from his stomach that he was hungry—he took into consideration that though Heather might also be hungry, she also wants to feel safe. Scott, taking a moment to recall the restaurants Heather liked, as well as focusing on her needs beyond the hunger pangs, demonstrated his love and care for her. This allowed her to feel safe in answering.

In order for a Piglet to walk in health, it requires that he fundamentally understand (and believe) that he is as valuable as anyone else. He needs to understand that he matters and that he doesn't have to apologize for his opinions or preferences. *Piglet often feels guilty for just having a preference.* Just as an unhealthy Owl desires order over healthy relationships, an unhealthy Piglet desires harmony over healthy relationships. Ironically, this eventually creates disharmony because no one knows what's really going on below the surface. Because of Piglet's ability to calm and soothe over a situation, on the surface, it masks all the angst and paddling that is going on below the water line. Tamping down conflict only serves to delay the inevitable. Piglet often assumes all responsibility for the conflict, so that no real resolution can be fully achieved unless Piglet allows others to paddle for themselves.

Connecting to the Source: Creatively Unique

*"Before I formed you in the womb I knew you, before you were born I set you apart; I appointed you as a prophet to the nations" (***Jeremiah 1:5 BSB).**

The scriptures make it clear that we are created beings with a purpose or destiny—there is thought and reason behind us being here. At the age of 17, God reveals to Jeremiah that even before he was conceived, God already had a blueprint or schematic of Jeremiah with a plan and purpose for his life.

Gondola Stop #4

Whoa! Look at that view! *Umm, it's kind of scary, but if you come along with me, I think I can do it*. And that's where we find Ruth. She's just lost her husband. She has no children. To top that all off, she has lost her brother-in-law, too. It's the worst news. Her mother-in-law, Naomi, had lost her husband ten years before and now her sons were gone. Naomi was away from her homeland of Bethlehem in Judea. She had gone to Moab with her husband and sons so many years before, because of famine in their land.

Now the famine in Bethlehem had ended. So, Naomi determined to go back home and to send her sons' wives to their respective homes, too. *But Ruth said no*. She determined to stay with Naomi, who changed her name to Mara, *because she was bitter*. Why did Ruth choose to go with a bitter woman? I think because she wanted Naomi to not be alone in her travels; in fact, she was determined to not only go, but to make Naomi's homeland and God her very own (which is an amazing way God would forge Ruth into the Bigger Story—it began with her caring concern and love for Naomi).

Only a Piglet would choose such a path. And we need our Piglets on the journey, because even though they might be fearful, they really are very brave underneath it all. And that bravery served Ruth well—she would marry a wonderful man, who loved her well. She would have a little, baby boy, which by the way would brighten the heart of Naomi, and then Ruth would become the great grandmother of King David...and be in the very line of Jesus, the King of Kings. *Talk about a Bigger Story!*

Five Signs You Need to Know Yourself and Others Better

1. When playing a new game will you break a rule that others don't know about?
2. While waiting in the express lane, do you have more than the 10 item limit, but reason that the two-one quart bottles of orange juice constitute one item?
3. Do you ever reorganize the dishwasher after someone else has already loaded it?
4. When you want to watch the missing disc from you LOTR collection and you know who has it, do you have a hard time asking them to return it?
5. Do you hold back your opinion on movie night, worrying others will not like it, even though you really want to watch the new Marvel movie?

Breaking It Down

Because Piglet has a high emotional IQ, he relies on his intuition rather than facts.

Sadly, in situations where Piglet's insights, information and input would greatly help bring resolution, he tends to remain silent. This is where his internal conversations go like this, "I may be right, but don't want to hurt/embarrass others who think they're right." While someone else is waxing eloquent and telling a story that you know to be completely implausible, Piglets will listen with rapt attention, never once questioning the story teller's integrity. If someone were to call out the storyteller, Piglet will simply say, *"Shhh... I want to hear what happens next."*

Similarly, Piglets have a hard time holding co-workers to accountability.

Even the most far-fetched and outlandish excuses a co-worker gives for not completing her project or assignment will have Piglet sympathizing with her and then offering to complete the assignment for her.

In childhood and adolescence, Piglets not only helped us with our homework, but they also probably did it. They allowed to us copy their test answers, let us eat part or all their lunch, and they never tattled on us--even taking the blame for what *we* did. To use a humorous illustration, you can easily spot a Piglet on an airplane because they are the one that's going up and down the aisle assisting everyone else to put on the oxygen masks that have dropped down from the overhead, but they are not wearing one themselves. The genesis of unhealthiness is when Piglet does not put on his own oxygen mask first. He can only help for a short while before his own need for oxygen is exhausted. Think of how many more people Piglet could have helped if he didn't run out of air!

These examples and explanations of an *unhealthy* Piglet describe that 96% of the American population. However, the New York Times' article did not refer to them as *Piglets*, it referred to them as *codependents*. When a Piglet is healthy, he retains all his caring and compassion toward others without causing damage to himself. By establishing and maintaining healthy boundaries*, Piglet will be empowered to actually help more people and for the right reasons. There is a difference.

Though his core need for harmony is the same, a healthy Piglet operates from a place of authentic generosity and real courage, while an unhealthy Piglet operates from a place of self-protection and crippling fear. Like that duck on the pond, while appearing magnanimous and full of comity on the surface, an unhealthy desire for harmony belies the ubiquitous inner battle beneath the waterline. This may sound harsh, but in truth, while an unhealthy Piglet may outwardly look generous, his self-protection and fear will cause him to act out of selfishness. An unhealthy Piglet has a habit of allowing, enabling or "putting up with" inappropriate behavior in others that he would never allow in himself. It takes unselfish courage to confront inappropriate behavior in family, friends and co-workers; but if Piglet wants harmony instead of healthy relationships, he will selfishly try to "keep the peace" rather than "make peace," so that Piglet will feel safe.

In any confrontation I try to always employ a *figurative* two-step approach. (Piglets effortlessly excel with step one and Owls effortlessly excel at step two). Both steps are needed and are not mutually exclusive in dealing with conflict. This figurative two-step approach is to first "put an arm around the shoulder of the person" and then "gently placing a finger on their chest". When administered correctly, the first step establishes that I'm with you and for you—that usually paves the way for the second step, which is to address the issue. If you're an Owl reading this paragraph... that "arm around the shoulder" part may have caused you to roll your eyes. And if you're a Piglet... that "finger in the chest" move may have caused you to reach for the Pepto Bismol®.

The tendency for a Piglet to become a codependent comes from seeking harmony for harmony's sake. *"Everyone just be nice; everyone just play fair; don't hurt anyone's feelings; everyone use your inside voices."* If Owl throws a flag on the play or blows his whistle, Piglet is quick to pick up the flag and hide it, so Owl can't throw it again. Piglet also will probably ask Owl to stop blowing the whistle, because it makes the players feel bad. A codependent's motto is, *"I'm okay as long as everyone else is okay, even if I'm not really okay,"* but in truth... *my dear Piglet*... that's not okay.

Only when a Piglet is healthy can he truly comfort people in affliction, encourage them in defeat and see the good in them without needing anything in return. A healthy Piglet doesn't need others to stop being mad or sad for him to feel safe. He doesn't automatically assume responsibility for other people's problems or moods.

Piglet also doesn't need to accommodate everyone's wishes—and certainly, he can choose a restaurant. A healthy Piglet's motto is, *"I'm okay with you not being okay,"* and in truth... *my dear Piglet*... that's totally okay!

In a Conflict

OWL
"I'm right."

RABBIT
"I'm right
(even if I'm not)."

PIGLET
"You're right
(even though
you're really not)."

TIGGER
"You're right."

Questions for Piglet:

1. Do you feel obligated to say "yes" when someone asks for a favor?
2. Do you usually assume responsibility for other's mistakes? that you are at fault?

Chapter Five: In Which Rabbit Takes Control of the Situation

"Organization is what you do before you do something, so that when you do it, it's not all mixed up."

A.A. Milne

If you are a Rabbit, you are in good company. Some of the greatest coaches, CEO's, entrepreneurs and inventors are Rabbits. Rabbits are the people that get things done in life, have a "can do" attitude and a "never say die" approach to any task.

If you are a Rabbit, you are a natural born leader. Rabbits have most, *if not all*, the answers. They are problem solvers and great at getting things accomplished on time or ahead of schedule. **In fact, Rabbits shine the brightest during times of chaos and crisis**. As they assume control over these situations or circumstances, the other characters will naturally line up behind--even without Rabbit even having to ask.

Sometimes Rabbits don't even need to or have the *right answer*, because for a lot of people who are in times of chaos and crisis, *any answer will do*. But even if the initial answer or solution they offer was not completely correct… **Rabbits have an uncanny way of continuing to lead until they come upon the correct solution**.

Here's an overview of Rabbit:

- Desires a controlled life and environment
- Values competency
- Processes using facts and their own experience
- Thinks and decides analytically
- Changes the rules
- Deals with conflict
- Always right (even when they're not)
- Tolerant of others
- Control = Self worth

Rabbits were born to be in charge or in control—it's their sweet-spot, and they are very good at it. They exude confidence and instill assurance in those they lead. But that confidence can erode quickly if their leadership is questioned or challenged. Remember that Rabbits hold competency (especially their own) in high regard, so when they are questioned or challenged, they have to fight against being dismissive of others (especially of those they don't deem as competent). That's why Rabbits usually are the ones who want to drive… well I'll tell you about that in more detail later in this chapter.

This tendency of Rabbits to take charge in times of crisis comes from an innate desire to "get everyone out alive!" Rabbits are very often what are referred to as "the hero" and are instinctively good at protecting others or leading them out of danger (for instance in alcoholic families, they will take charge to help the other siblings). In addition, they have a lot of confidence in their own abilities, experiences and talents. However, they generally do not have as much confidence in those around them.

For some Rabbits there doesn't even have to be any crisis for them to take over. It's difficult for some Rabbits to watch someone struggling to accomplish what they deem as *a simple task*. After watching them struggle for a few minutes, a Rabbit might say, "Move," or "Just hand it to me," and they take over and accomplish the task. For instance, you may have experienced or seen this before when a teenager might take their parent's smart phone to resolve the problem that parent is facing with a sigh of impatience at the parent's ignorance and slowness with technology.

To understand Rabbit, you need to know that they place a high value on competency. They expect it of themselves and respect it in others. They have a desire to live a life of control. Rabbits don't like to appear incompetent, and they struggle unless they have things and situations under control. Sometimes, this equates to Rabbits tendency to control others. Note: order and control are similar in some respects but are two very different needs.

Assessments, suggestions or corrections offered by others can fall on deaf ears if Rabbit feels threatened or doesn't trust the messenger. However, when sufficiently shown their mistakes and effectively corrected, Rabbits can be extremely grateful and have a newfound respect for the one who brought correction. Why? Well because that person just made Rabbit even more competent. The trick is, while being corrected, Rabbits are probably thinking to themselves, "Is this person competent enough to correct me?"

Elijah's Story: *"For which of you, desiring to build a tower, does not sit down and count the cost, whether he has enough to complete it" (***Luke 14:28 ESV).**

"I'm so stupid," Elijah said with his chin on his chest. "I'm nineteen years old, and I still don't know how to change the oil in my car." Watching Elijah wringing his hands, as he spoke, and rarely looking up was painful for me. This is a good kid, who really tries. Since I'd been in Elijah's life for about six years, I asked him a question, "Did anyone ever teach you how to do an oil change?" Looking up he replied, "Yeah, my dad tried to teach me a bunch of times, but I'm just too stupid to get it." I smiled and said, "Elijah you are anything but stupid, and I think you were taught how to do an oil change by a Rabbit." Elijah looked at me with hopeful tears in his eyes because he knew exactly what I meant. Elijah had been on a humanitarian relief trip with me and had taken the "Who the Pooh are You?" test as part of the training.

"Your dad's a Rabbit, isn't he?" I asked. Leaning back in his chair Elijah chuckled, "Oh my gosh, my dad is a huge Rabbit! In fact, he's all Rabbit!" I was so happy that a simple test that Elijah took when he was a sophomore in high school now served him as a freshman in college to better understand himself (and his dad).

Elijah was 12 years old, when his dad first tried to teach him how to change the oil in a car. That day his father's Rabbit side came out in a big way. His dad knew how to change the oil and how long it should take. With all the patience of a seagull waiting on a bread crumb, Elijah's dad barked out commands that made Elijah tense up, and he feared making a mistake. To add to his anxiety, he either didn't have the strength or the finesse to remove the oil filter.

While straining and grunting his hand repeatedly slipped off the oil filter wrench—and eventually after what seemed like the millionth time, his dad said what a lot of Rabbits say and do in situations like this. Elijah's dad crawled under the car next to his son and grumbled, "Just move;" and with his meaty hand grasping the oil filter wrench, his dad was able to loosen the oil filter in his first attempt. Elijah told me it was then that he "felt like a failure".

I'm sure you can sympathize with Elijah, after all he was just a kid and if you think back... you may recall being in similar situations. But before taking Elijah's side and assuming his dad was a big jerk, I want to help you understand his dad a little more.

Rabbit wants to teach his son a life skill. He's purchased the oil, the filter and has all the tools needed to perform a task that he's been doing for years. Dad knows how long it will take to change the oil and is confident in his ability to properly use the oil filter wrench. But Rabbit is not an Owl and didn't take the time to consider all the factors and variables when adding a twelve-year-old to the mix. Dad set aside the proper amount of time it usually took for an oil change, but when he decided that today is the day to teach his son how to change the oil... he most likely didn't add any additional time for giving instructions or helping correct mistakes.

Rabbit wants to get things done—and usually as quickly as possible. And though dad truly loves his son and genuinely wants to teach him how to change the oil, Rabbit needed to first "count the cost" of inviting an extra set of inexperienced hands.

Before moving on, who do you most identify with in this story?

- You might be a parent or grandparent and yet identify more with Elijah. Are there things or tasks that you have never been good at because maybe you were never really taught how to do them?

- You might be a teenager or young adult and yet identify with his dad. Are there times when you've been trying to teach someone how to do something and ultimately for the sake of expediency just did it yourself?

It's real-life scenarios like these where we all have the opportunity to discover if we are a healthy version of our personality-type or one that still has some work to do. Because teaching Elijah how to change the oil required patience more than just knowing how to do it.

Patience Please: Rabbits as Coaches and Teachers

Rabbits often make great coaches and *can become* amazing teachers. Coaches have a way of getting more out of an athlete than they ever expected of themselves. When people want to quit or give up, Rabbits have the innate ability to see potential and what that person is capable of. They won't let others quit and will push, prod or stretch them into achieving what was once unobtainable. Rabbits inspire and cultivate greatness in others because they expect it of themselves.

If you played sports, can you recall the coaches in your life? I would wager that the best coach you ever had believed in you when you couldn't believe in yourself. They pushed you to your limits, and there you found you could go even further. And I'll bet that the best coach you ever had taught you the value of praising others for a win and taking sole ownership for the loss. Rabbits often make great coaches... and they can also become amazing teachers. What's the difference between a coach and a teacher and why do you keep saying *"can become* amazing teachers"? I am so glad you keep asking these great questions *or at least you keep reading these great questions*.

The main difference I see between a coach and a teacher is that a coach helps athletes focus on their own individual greatness turn their focus toward achieving greatness as part of a team. A teacher is someone with a classroom of students, who helps each student achieve individual academic success.

Being a good teacher takes more than just having a working knowledge of the subject at hand, legible penmanship on the white board and not being boring. Being a good teacher requires something that Rabbit is not necessarily known for—patience. Patience is a learned self-discipline or as the Apostle Paul refers to it... *the fruit of the Spirit*.

Patience is not the first word that comes to mind when describing a Rabbit. As a matter of fact, Larry the Cable Guy's famous catch phrase, *"Git'r done!"* would be an appropriate bumper sticker for Rabbit. Expediency is not the only thing a Rabbit appreciates; remember the word competency is still in play with Rabbit, and often+

times they view competency as doing things the way that they do or seeing things the way they see them.

In a teaching or learning environment, the teacher's goal is to **teach** in such a way that the student **learns** how to do it. It's not rocket science, but this simple point often escapes many of us when in the midst of teaching we just want to *git'r done*.

If a Rabbit will <u>*consider the cost*</u>, *slow down* and allow for a few mistakes, the end result is so much better for both parties. Rabbit doesn't have to actually do any of the work. In the end, the student doesn't feel defeated or believe that they are a failure.

I'm curious, if anyone reading this chapter may be starting to connect a few dots and realize that they too may have been taught by a Rabbit, and that's the reason you never really understood Algebra... never learned how to change a tire or how to play chess. I wonder, too, if anyone reading this feels compelled to help their child to see how X really equals Y... or maybe invite them out to the garage... maybe even pull out the chess board... **and try, try again**.

On Owls and Rabbits

Rabbits *can become* wonderful teachers. And yet... they can be some of the worst teachers on the planet! Why? Because while Owl wants to get it done the right way,

Rabbit wants to get it done their way. Remember that Owl is a "Ready... aim... aim... aim... aim..." type. Rabbit is a "Ready FIRE aim!" type. Owl measures twice (usually more) and cuts once (because there's a lumber budget). Rabbit measured once (on a previous project) and cuts as many times as it takes to get it right (because we can always buy more wood). Owl follows the rules, Piglet bends the rules and Rabbit changes them.

By their nature Rabbits are typically competitive, so they don't like losing-- in fact, they hate it. Though they are similar in some ways, here's where Owls' and Rabbits' order and control start to differ. While playing a board game, **Owl not only knows the rules, but Owl also obeys them**. Sitting right next to Owl, playing the same board game...**it's not uncommon for Rabbit to change or break the rules in their quest to win**. They may even make up a rule in the middle of the game that no one has ever heard of before. Although Rabbit may change or even break the rules, they can't stand it if others do the same.

Both Owl and Rabbit like to get things accomplished. When it comes to a home repair project Owl wants to get it done right while Rabbit wants to get it done right now. Owl will take the time to research what needs to be done, watch an instructional video, clarify their role or responsibilities, discover what proper tools are required and how long the project will take. Rabbit will just hit it with a hammer.

Rabbits Being Rabbits

But seriously, if expediency is the most valuable measure of a task or a project, then enlist Rabbit because **Rabbit will get it done now**. If there's no pressing deadline but staying on or under budget is the most important, then put Owl in charge because not only will it be done right, but it will also stay well under budget. If your main concern is the care and well-being of your staff during the project, then Piglet is your best bet to manage the team. And If for some crazy reason, the only purpose of the project to is to have fun, then it's Tigger time! But we'll learn all about Tigger soon enough.

Again, competency is extremely important to Rabbit so losing an argument can be as unsettling as losing a game. As we discovered that while playing games Rabbits may change, break or make up rules if they are losing**. So, it's feasible that when Rabbit is in the midst of losing an argument they may be tempted to alter or even make up facts.** This is why Rabbit will come across as always being right... even when they're not.

Though they don't particularly enjoy it, some Rabbits can admit when they are wrong and gratefully accept and appreciate corrected information while other Rabbits will die on any hill to win an argument. They will work to convince you that the sky is down, and that the Pope is really a Methodist. It's fun to listen to two Rabbits argue sports. Neither one has a truly "unbiased" point of view, because their team is the best. A close call at home plate will have both of them intently watching the exact same replay in slow motion multiple times but will be completely divided. One sees the runner is clearly safe at home while the other sees the runner is clearly out. To be fair, every character has this same tendency to see life through their lens of choice, but **Rabbits can be relentless and will sometimes hang on long after everyone else has moved on to the next inning**.

What might surprise you is that Rabbits are **not** ones who seek conflict. **They are happy not to have to deal with conflict, because conflict involves dealing with other people's problems**. While accomplishing a task or working on a project, Rabbit hopes to keep drama at arm's length and just keeps on trucking. However, if the conflict arrives on their doorstep, they will take control and make decisions to end, but not necessarily *resolve* the conflict. When working with people, the potential for conflict will always be there—and remember, Rabbits don't take sides; they just take over.

This full-steam-ahead approach may lead a Rabbit to run over people who are, in Rabbit's view, moving too slowly or standing in the way, but not and I repeat, not with the intention to do harm. They just want to get the job done. After a project is completed, a Rabbit will often send out thank you notes and gift cards to their team members, who during the project thought Rabbit was being mean and heartless. On the contrary, they were just focused on finishing. By the way, don't expect a note or gift card from an Owl, because gift cards weren't in the budget.

On the Job...er...Mission Trip Training

Since **Who the Pooh are You?** started out as a way to help middle and high school students understand themselves and others while on mission trips, I thought it appropriate to share a Rabbit story from one of those trips. This was a high school trip.

When I assembled teams for mission trips, I had a two-pronged approach. First, I extended an open-ended invitation for volunteers. Second, I recruited specific individuals for the trip. There was a particular student I had in mind for a trip to Mexico in 2004 and was really hoping that her Rabbit father would want to come, as well. I was thrilled when both Jenny* and her dad, Leon*, signed up (* Names have been changed to protect the innocent.).

Leon was a godsend. He knew all about construction; and since we would be building houses in one of the poorest areas in Mexico, his addition to the team made me look really smart. Leon was a good leader, organizer and was especially good at supporting me as the leader of the trip. At pre-field orientation and during every team training session prior to the trip, I knew I could depend on Leon for anything. We divided our main team into seven smaller teams that would each build one house for a family in Reynosa.

The goal of the mission trip was to build a relationship with the family **first** and then to build them a house. This one detail about which came first was when Leon's Rabbit side became evident.

Remember that Rabbit wants to get things done and done now. *"We can have fun later, but now we work."* Well... that whole "build a relationship first" thing made Leon feel like he was wearing a shirt made of hair. Leon wanted to build the house first, and then get to the relationship part. We were three days into a five-day build when I walked around to each build site to see how each team was coming along. The houses were all within walking distance but spread out over a large community.

As I approached Leon's site, I took out my camera and took a photo from about 100 feet away. When I got to the house, Leon was on the roof with two students sweating it out as they rolled out, tacked and tarred the rolled-roofing shingle, while some of his team were on the ground handing up cups of water and supplies, as needed. I called up to Leon and asked him to come down from the roof and take a break. While feverishly working to get the roof finished before the end of the day, Leon was, shall we say, a bit reluctant to honor my request. "Leon! I need your help!" I called out. He stopped what he was doing, surveyed how much was left to do, gave some instructions to the boys on the roof and begrudgingly climbed down the ladder (it was a ladder, in theory) and accepted the cup of water I extended to him. "Come on Leon, walk with me," I said, as he guzzled the first of several cups of water.

Leon and I chit-chatted, as we wandered away from his site, all while glancing back over his shoulder to make sure his team was continuing the work. "Hey man, look at this photo I just took," I said, as I handed Leon my digital camera. Leon broke off his gaze from his worksite to focus on the photo. After adjusting the camera and shading it with his hand, so that he could see it in the ubiquitous sunshine, I asked him, "How would you caption that pic?" Leon's eyes filled with tears, as he looked at the image, and then back at his team in the distance. "Mary and Martha," he replied.

Leon was referring to a well-known story from the Bible about when Jesus came to a town to visit some friends who were sisters. While one sister was sitting at Jesus' feet in the living room listening to Him talk, the other was in the kitchen preparing food, food that He didn't even ask for. While Mary just sat there doing nothing, Martha became increasingly irritated that she was left to prep the food, all alone. Suddenly Martha appeared in the living room and let Mary have it... by yelling at Jesus. (I would have loved to have been there to see this). What Jesus says to Martha is quite interesting and full of insight for Rabbits to ponder. *"Martha, Martha," He replied, "You are worried and upset about many things, but only one thing is worth being concerned about and Mary has discovered it...."* The lesson for Leon that day was what he saw on my camera.

From about 100 feet away, the photo showed a house under construction, a group of 15 people wearing matching t-shirts and small group of about 7 children. A closer look revealed three of those wearing the matching t-shirts were on the roof, two of them were on the ground handing up supplies and 10 were laughing, playing and loving 7 little ones.

Leon had been so focused on getting the house finished, he missed out getting to know the people he was building it for! Martha was so busy in the kitchen preparing a meal she missed out on spending time with the person she was making it for.

Trusting others is a challenge for most Rabbits. They know their own talents and capabilities but are not so sure of others. That's why it seems like Rabbits are trying to control things. My friend Leon wasn't being a jerk or a control freak—he, like a lot of Rabbits, have a difficult time trusting others to do things the way (or in the timeframe) they want them accomplished. Learning to trust others is a good first step in becoming a healthier Rabbit.

Having Rabbit around brings a lot of security and assurance to organizations and to families. You can trust Rabbit to get things done, find quick solutions to problems, make a plan, act decisively and then adjust any flaw in their plan along the way.

It's a Matter of Trust. In a counseling session with Crystal (Rabbit) and Dan (Owl), the issue of who should drive came up. Apparently, this had become a highly contentious issue between them and often resulted in them arriving at their destination not speaking to each other—exhausted from the arguments that occupied their entire drive. Crystal was insistent that she should drive all the time, while Dan felt that since he was a professional truck driver, the driving duties should naturally fall to him. On the occasions when Dan would drive, Crystal would criticize Dan's choice of route, the speed he would go and call his braking unacceptable. Dan would fight back that he knew what he was doing, was only obeying speed limits and that there was nothing wrong with his braking. What Dan didn't know was why Crystal always wanted to drive—neither did Crystal until I asked her some questions.

The first question I asked Crystal was (in my humble opinion, absolutely brilliant!) "Why do you always want to drive?" (I told you it was brilliant!) The look on her face told me that she had never been asked that question before. She looked over to Dan seemingly for help, but he just shrugged his shoulders and looked at me. Crystal was at a loss for an answer, so I asked her another. "Crystal, do you trust Dan's driving?" and without hesitation she emphatically replied "No!" She went on to relay a story about a near-boating accident that had happened years earlier (while they were just dating) with Dan at the helm. They were both new to boating, so it was decided that Dan would pilot the small vessel. Dan made a simple mistake that could have been disastrous, but fortunately the other boat's driver was experienced and saved them all from peril. Crystal never forgot.

As Crystal was recalling the boating accident, it was clear that Dan was embarrassed and became defensive reminding Crystal that it was his "first time piloting a boat" and that he's much better now... and besides... that happened on a boat, we were talking about driving a car.

But the issue wasn't about the boat or a car, it was about trust.

Crystal's need for control came from a lack of trust—a result of Dan's lack of boating experience that caused a near catastrophe. Crystal's response was absolutely normal for a Rabbit, "Oh my gosh.... the boat's out of control, and we're all going to die!" This left a deep impression on Crystal's psyche, and she reasoned that she was no longer safe with Dan behind the wheel of anything—be it a boat or a car.

Crystal trusted her driving, but she had an experience and a reason not to trust Dan's driving. After the near catastrophe, it was now up to Rabbit to take control of the driving duties and make sure that everyone in the car arrives alive. It was now Dan's turn to answer some questions.

"Dan, do you think that Crystal's need to drive is because she's just control freak or maybe... just maybe... the boating incident caused her to become fearful when you're driving anything, including the car?" Dan thought for a moment and said, "Yeah I can see that." I turned to Crystal and asked, "Do you think that when Dan is driving the car, that your criticism could be because you don't trust his driving the boat?" Crystal paused for several seconds before sighing, "Yes, but I was soon to discover that Crystal's need for control went deeper than the boating trauma.

Crystal began telling me about her past before she ever met Dan and that some of her previous relationships with other men greatly contributed to her need to control Dan.

Because of past hurts, betrayals and disappointments, Crystal's solution was to be in control not just of who drove the car, but in every aspect their relationship. Her mindset was that in order to not be in another bad relationship was to control her relationship with Dan, which ironically just made for yet another bad relationship. She was in control, but in control of a bad relationship. By the way... controlling your spouse, friends, family or co-workers is not good for relationships.

I asked her if she trusted Dan to be a faithful husband. Again, she paused for several seconds (which caused Dan some anxiety) before replying,

"Yes, yes I really do. He's a good man and I hate myself for fussing at him... even while I'm doing it. In my head I'm telling myself to stop, but I just keep doing it."

I assured Crystal that is a common trait among all personality-types to be aware (even in the moment) that we are doing or saying something we wished we were not doing or saying, but sometimes that train has left the station with no brakes.

Dan and Crystal are doing much better now. When Dan drives, instead of ignoring the Rabbit in Crystal, he will enquire which route she prefers to travel. He also lets her pick the music. When Crystal has a preferred route, she will tell Dan; but more often than not, she'll defer to Dan and say, "I trust you to get us there." Dan even told me recently that she occasionally lets him choose the music.

The goal of this book is to help every character be the best version of that character they can be. The overview or bullet point list of each character is designed to provide a simple way to understand each character, but other than that you may have noticed that there is not a template or formula used in describing each character. For instance, in explaining Owl, the writing style and examples used were different than those used for Piglet. This was to not only explain Owl to others, but Owl to another Owl, as well. To help a Rabbit to (not only) identify their personality, but it is also equally important for them to discover how their personality (healthy or unhealthy) impacts those around them. This unique approach to reveal each character has been repeated for each of the characters you've met thus far.

Connecting to the Source: You are in Your Family, but you are Not Your Family

Just because everyone in your family has always been academically inclined doesn't mean that you or your child or your future grandchildren will be. You or your child may excel in other areas that have not been associated with your family tree. Musical talent may suddenly appear in a family member where that particular talent has never manifested before.

And because you were born into a family with a long history of athleticism doesn't mean that you or your children will excel at sports. Imagine a 6'5" high school freshman shows up on the first day of school. Because of their height we most likely make some quick assumptions and conclude the obvious.

The basketball coach with dreams of a state championship in his eyes approaches the jolly green freshman and asks, "Hey, are you going to try out for the basketball team this year?" Imagine the coach's disappointment if the student replied, "No thanks coach, I'm joining the art club... I want to be a painter and specialize in ceilings." The poor coach sadly walks away shaking his head bemoaning the waste of talent. What if that kid had absolutely no athletic abilities and was just really tall?

In order to get the most out of this book, it's important to process the information with not only your mind, but with your heart, soul and spirit as well. Only reading this for information is not going to be that helpful. This will be just another book that you read and some more information that you've acquired. I invite you to utilize the emotional and spiritual components that we are all given to gain a fuller understanding.

Because we often view people through our natural eyes long before engaging our spiritual eyes (2 Corinthians 5:16), we see people the way we see them and not necessarily the way God does.

Gondola Stop #5

The Bigger Story and its ramifications are really flabbergasting. Just like the view we see from up high, there is so much to take in – the details alone are beyond our comprehension--***but not for God.*** God can see the end of the timeline from the beginning. As Hebrews 12:2 states, He is the Author and Finisher of our faith. He knows it, and He invites us to choose to come alongside Him in it. (He also knows what we will choose, which is mind-blowing!) In the Bigger Story, we make some amazing choices that have an impact that goes way beyond our knowing. All the while, God is in the smallest of details That is where we find Moses...in a basket on the Nile.

Pharaoh had ordered that all Hebrew baby boys be killed. So, Moses' mother made a basket out of papyrus and sent his sister to place him on the river in it. His sister waits by the shore, watching to see that he will be safely found. He is! And, of all people, by the daughter of Pharaoh herself! He would then be fed by his own Hebrew mother until he was weaned and brought back to Pharaoh's daughter, who named him Moses. He would grow up in Pharaoh's household and learn the ways of the Egyptians in a primo spot. As a young man, Moses would know enough about his heritage to be quite angry when an Egyptian was beating a Hebrew, angry enough to kill the abuser. Upon hearing that someone saw it happen and that Pharaoh heard and was going to kill him, he fled to Midian.

In Midian, Moses would defend seven women from shepherds that would not let them water their flocks. After defending them, he watered the flocks himself. Later, he married one of the women, a woman named Zipporah. Moses would become a father and grow in wisdom under his wife's father, who was a priest of Midian. Moses would be close to 80 years old when he saw the burning bush of God. Here God would lay out instructions for Moses' next assignment and promise to go with him.

Amazingly Moses would walk in this calling, ushering all the Hebrew slaves out of Egypt, as the waters of the Red Sea parted, allowing God's people to pass through. After they were safely across, the waters swallowed up the entire army of Pharaoh! The people would begin their journey towards their promised land. Of course, they would doubt God sinfully and their children would be the ones to inherit that promised land—except for two of the OG's (original God's-men--*grin*), Caleb and Joshua. But on this journey, God would show Moses details of the life the Israelites would live, so that he could lead God's people well.

For, you see, Moses is a Rabbit. He was born and set-apart to lead God's people out of Egypt. And yes, he would break some rules, which would greatly mark his journey—both in fleeing to Midian from murdering the Egyptian and in not getting to enter the Promised Land of Canaan, because he disobeyed God (where he was supposed to speak to, *not tap*, the rock for water).

But, God greatly loved Moses. He spoke with Moses, face to face, as you do with a friend. He listened to Moses and even let him glimpse Canaan from a mountain top. He would be buried in a secret place. And in fact, Moses would be seen in the New Testament up on a mountain with Jesus, Elijah, Peter, James and John. Oh, to have a glimpse into that scene and to hear their discussion! ***Glorious***!

The Bigger Story here is filled with the smallest, but quite important, details. Each part fit together into a whole that would show that God prepared it perfectly for Moses to carry out. While Moses learned much in his environments, he really relied on God's leading one day a time. God would even send Moses good counsel through his father-in-law to judge the people's many disputes. I tell you what, a man like Moses is tailor-made for such trials that he endured and overcame—and it all started in an infant's basket on the Nile!

Here are Five Signs You Need to Get to Know Yourself and Others Better

1. While waiting in the "express" 10 items or less checkout lane, do you count the items in other people's shopping carts?
2. When something needs repair, do you initially wonder if it's your fault, have trouble deciding what to do and ask other people what they would do?
3. When you notice the missing disc in your LOTR (*Lord of the Rings*) collection do you contact the person who has it or just order a new one?
4. Do chips and cracks mysteriously appear on dishes and glassware after you load the dishwasher?
5. When something needs repair, do you think about what proper tools are required and if there is a DIY video?

Now it's time to meet our fourth and final character. "Bouncy, bouncy, bouncy, bouncy, fun, fun, fun, fun,

fun… the most wonderful thing about a Tigger… is when they finally leave your house.”

Chapter Six: In Which Tigger Bowls Everyone Over

"Oh Tigger, where are your manners?"
"I don't know, but I bet they're having more fun than I am."

A.A. Milne

"Anyone who listens to the Word but does not do what it says is like a person who looks at their face in a mirror and after looking at themselves goes away and immediately forgets what they look like" **(James 1:24 NIV).**

If you are a Tigger, you've probably been described as *energetic, fun or spontaneous* among other words that we'll get to later. Tiggers are naturally adept at being around strangers and new situations. Tiggers have no problem with a change of plans or doing something *last minute*--in fact, they enjoy it. They are quick to make friends and will attest to having lots of them. Tiggers are usually the life of any party and, unless there is another Tigger present, are often the center of attention. Tiggers are creative, quick on their feet and have a reputation for loquaciously sharing their feelings and opinions on almost every subject.

Tiggers derive energy from being around people (especially new people) and are very accepting, engaging and wildly entertaining. When meeting new people, because Tiggers typically *wear their heart on their sleeve,* they will often get the feeling that *they've known the person (that they just met) their whole life* and dive headfirst into new friendships and relationships.

Being accepting of others, Tiggers try to see both sides of an argument. Even if they have determined who is right and who is wrong, they still try to see where each person is coming from and can alter the mood of contentious situations.

It's been said that some people are like thermometers, they adjust to the temperature around them. Tiggers on the other hand are the thermostats of the world, as they adjust the temperature to suit them. In situations where it's starting to feel *a little chilly,* Tiggers have an unequaled ability to lighten the mood and warm things back up. And if a situation is starting to get *a little heated,* they have an uncanny way of cooling everyone down.

Tiggers are good at accepting others, but don't think for one second that they don't want the same kind of acceptance. Tiggers need what they freely offer to others and if this need for acceptance goes unmet, Tiggers can get into trouble.

Tiggers are also known for being late or not showing up at a party… and if they do finally show up, they've forgotten the birthday cake that they promised to pick up on their way to the party… more about that later.

Like the other characters, Tigger is often misunderstood by others. And because of Tiggers' typical behavior, they don't do themselves any favors clearing up misconceptions.

Since Tigger is typically energetic, spontaneous, the center of attention, loquacious, maybe a little too quick to make friends, rarely if ever on time and enjoys changing your plans it stands to reason that just a tiny bit of Tigger can go a very long way with an Owl or a Rabbit.

One way to describe Tigger is that they are the "nutmeg" in the spice rack of life. I'm sure you're already familiar with nutmeg, as it is commonly used in pumpkin pies as well as being one of the things you can sprinkle into your coffee at Starbucks®. Not only does nutmeg have a unique and distinctive taste, but nutmeg is also found to have health benefits that include pain relief, easing indigestion, improving circulation and increasing the immune system--just to name a few. Betcha some of you didn't know that. Nutmeg has more to offer than what it appears… just like Tiggers.

Though nutmeg is a common spice, and most people like it, nutmeg is not used every day or in most recipes. Have you ever noticed while eating in a restaurant that there is usually salt and pepper shakers on each table? But have you ever seen a nutmeg shaker (not including Starbucks®) on your table? I think not.

Another thing about nutmeg is that it can overpower other spices. Just a little nutmeg goes a very long way. Remember that in some recipes, sugar is measured by the cup while nutmeg is almost always measured in fractions of a teaspoon.

Tigger's spontaneity can be problematic at times because unlike Owl, schedules, details and margin are not very important to Tigger. That's why it's not uncommon for a Tigger to "over commit and under deliver" and to have accepted multiple different party invitations for the same night.

When given an invitation to a party, Owls rely on their "the five w's" to process the decision (as to whether or not) to attend a party. After checking their calendar and taking the time needed for consideration, Owl will then accept or decline the invitation.

The details don't usually cross a Tiggers mind because Tiggers rarely hear anything after, "You want to come to my party?" They have a tendency to quickly accept party invitations and even agree to bring something needed before hearing the details. While the person is giving the details, Tigger is otherwise occupied mentally picturing what they are going to wear and thinking about who else might be at the party.

Everyone knows a Tigger and they are very easy to identify because they love attention. Not all attention though, they just want the good and affirming kind.

Here's a snapshot of Tigger

- Accepting of others
- Desires other's acceptance and fun
- Processes using their feelings and gut instincts
- Thinks and decides emotionally
- There's rules? (*sic*)
- Avoids conflict
- Occasionally right
- Needs others
- Acceptance = Self worth

In a Conflict

OWL
"I have things to do and places to be."

PIGLET
"Are they okay? Are they angry? Are they angry with me? How can I make them stop being angry?"

RABBIT
"I know the best way to do things and what's best for this person."

TIGGER
"I want to be this person's favorite!"

If you know a Tigger, they may have a reputation for being insincere and undependable. In truth they are quite genuine, but **highly impulsive**. The most-likely reason that Tigger didn't show up at your house at 5:30pm to give you a ride to the airport is because they had several other offers to do something at 5:30pm that same day and forgot their commitment to you... especially if their other offers were more fun than a trip to the airport. When Tigger doesn't show up at planned meeting or event, when they don't complete a task or fulfill an obligation, it would be easy to assume that they were insincere when they accepted the request and completely unreliable when committing to a project.

Because Tigger desires the acceptance of others, he, like Piglet, has a hard time saying, "no," but for very different reasons. Piglet doesn't want to hurt someone's feelings; Tigger just wants someone to like him. So, if you ask Tigger to give you a ride to the airport, his initial response is to accommodate your request; but be forewarned, if you ask for a ride to the airport several days in advance, you run the risk of Tigger not showing up at 5:30pm like they said they would. Why? Because Tiggers usually have a lot of friends and acquaintances (that they consider friends) Your "well in advance" request gives an opportunity for Tigger to get a better offer for next Tuesday at 5:30pm. When Tigger agreed to take you to the airport, they sincerely intended to take you... in the moment. However, when asking a Tigger to be somewhere at a certain time, you might want to ask them in this way.

"Hey Tigger, are you free to give me a ride to the airport next Tuesday at 5:30pm?
Are you sure?
Did you check your calendar?
Why don't you call your wife just to make sure?"

Why all the follow up questions, you might ask? Because here in bold type is what's going on inside of Tigger.

"Hey Tigger, are you free to give me a ride to the airport next Tuesday at 5:30pm?" **Yes.** "Are you sure?" **Absolutely.** "Did you check your calendar" **What**

calendar? *"Why don't you call your wife just to make sure."* **You mean right now?**

If you are a Tigger, and someone asks you to do something or be somewhere in the absence of your spouse or partner, for the love of Pete and all that is holy, call home immediately! Tigger loves spontaneity, and typically has only a vague idea of their schedule beyond the present moment, and as a result, Tigger (*at best*) simply knows that it's starting to get dark outside.

If someone asked you who your favorite teacher was back in elementary, junior or high school, the answer would mostly likely be a teacher that was a Tigger. *Why?* Because that teacher made learning fun, they accepted you for who you were and every test he gave was "multiple choice" or as Tigger would say, "multiple guess." Tiggers make for great teachers, entertainers and excel at customer service. And like Rabbit, a healthy Tigger makes a great coach. Tiggers have an instinctual gift for gathering, inspiring and empowering people, so that once a task is accomplished or a project is completed, everyone involved can't wait for the next project to start. Tigger has a way of making everyone on the team feel special and that they are Tigger's number one favorite. No matter how arduous or mundane the task, Tigger will find a component of fun... and because he is typically very creative, Tigger can create a complex game with just a piece of string and a clothespin. Tiggers can also be competitive and will often bend or break the rules in order to win, but most often they violate the rules just so that *everyone is having fun*.

Tigger sees the positive in people and believes that everyone is basically good. He is often surprised when someone hurts or disappoints him, because he would never **purposely** hurt or disappoint anyone else. He tends to be blindly loyal and like Piglet, will allow others to violate healthy boundaries because... well... Tiggers (unless they are healthy) have never met a boundary that they didn't violate themselves.

Tigger did not intend to hurt or disappoint you by not taking you to the airport. He simply forgot. Tigger had every intention of picking you up, but unless you kept reminding Tigger of their commitment, even up to just a couple of hours before they were to arrive, it can safely be assumed that being at your house at 5:30pm on Tuesday is not at the forefront of his mind. Because of Tigger's tendency to focus on the here and now and being in the moment, whoever Tigger is with and whatever Tigger is doing at 5:00pm on Tuesday is the most important thing.

It is important to note that it's actually **not** what Tiggers are currently doing, who they are currently with or that they're having more fun than a drive to the airport would be... It boils down to Tiggers' need for **acceptance** from the person they are currently with that becomes the most important thing. Given the choice between being accepted, having fun or being dependable, Tigger will almost always choose the former over the latter two.

What can be maddening for others and for Tigger himself, actually, is an unawareness or understanding of why they behave this way. What I've observed in Tigger behavior (especially in children) is a pattern of thinking in which "If they think it, they did it." If you believe that one of your children might be a Tigger, here's a little test.

If you notice that the trash is piling up in your kitchen trash can and resembles a strange version of the game Jenga®, call to the child you think is a Tigger (this even works on grown-ups) that's in another room and ask, *"James, will you take the kitchen trash out?"* His response will mostly likely be, *"Yes mommy!"* or *"Okay dad!"*. Now don't say another word about taking out the trash. Then after about 45 minutes or so, call to them again and ask, *"James, did you take the trash out?"* They will most likely respond with, *"Yes!"* or *"Uh huh!"* And yet, there you stand, staring at that same smelly version of Jenga® wondering why your child is lying to you. May I suggest that they are not lying, but because of the way they think and process... simply put--"if they **thought it**... they **did it**."

Tiggers are creative and highly imaginative, so that most often results in them being very visual in the way they process. They process with mental images, so Tiggers learn best by utilizing pictures rather than words. Before assembling a piece of furniture, Owl reads the directions, lays out all the parts and counts out all the hardware before he would even consider starting. Tigger looks at the photo on the outside of the box and dives in headfirst. And after the assembly is complete, he assumes that any leftover parts, hardware or shelving are just extras.

When you asked Tigger to take out the trash (that was in the kitchen), because they were in another room and **not** in the kitchen when you asked... while still doing whatever they were doing when you asked, Tigger will process your request by visualizing the trash can in the kitchen, as well as visualizing themselves getting the trash (that's still in the kitchen), and taking it out to the garbage can at the curb. Again, because they "thought it" they "saw themselves doing it" and when you ask if they did it, they answer without hesitation, *"Yup!"*

Now it's your turn to be a healthy version of your character.

- An unhealthy Piglet will probably just take the trash out themselves.

- An unhealthy Rabbit may stand next to the trashcan demanding they take it out now.

- And an unhealthy Owl may accuse Tigger of lying.

Here's another way a handling this situation.

Whether you are a Piglet, Owl, Rabbit (or even another Tigger yourself) fight the temptation to just do it yourself, go stand in the doorway, so Tigger can see you as well as hear you and without fussing, cussing or accusing, ask Tigger to come into the kitchen. As he enters the kitchen, simply point to the trashcan and without any harshness in your voice ask, *"Are you sure you took out the trash?"* Now step back and get ready to be amazed. Remember that Tigger wants acceptance, which also means they just want you to like them.

When Tigger lays eyes on the still not yet emptied trashcan, invariably he will gasp with wide-eyed surprise, quickly gather up the trash and run it out to the garbage can at the curb. And when he comes back inside, he will often ask, *"Is there any else you want me to do?"* Why? Because taking out the trash pleased you, and now that he is in kitchen *and in the moment,* his desire for acceptance will lead him to do even more for you, because that will make you like Tigger even more. However, if an Owl, Piglet or Rabbit are unhealthy in dealing with situations like these, it actually serves to sour the relationship with Tigger-- he may give up trying to ever please you again.

Tiggers will often make up for a lack of skills or talent with their personality. Playing golf in a foursome with three players, who take their game a little too seriously (unless you are on the PGA or LPGA tours... lighten up a bit), and a Tigger who just plays for the fun of it, as an interesting case study. The issue of Tigger not taking the game seriously will cause blood pressures of the other three to rise; and he may end up at the end of 9 holes, walking back to the clubhouse alone, while the three ride off in the golf carts to play the back nine. Unless Tigger is taking their shot, the boredom of waiting his turn will have them goofing off in the sightline of the other golfers and when called out, he may respond by making up a song and dancing to it.

Golfer:
"Hey, can you move? You're in my sightline."
Tigger:
"I'm in your sightline, I'm in your sightline."
Golfer:
"Stop it!"
Tigger:
"They said to stop it... they said to stop it..."
Golfer:
"Knock it off or I'm gonna hit you with my club!"
Tigger:
"They're gonna kill me... they're gonna kill me..."

Sound familiar?

Tigger wants to please, be liked and desires to be the center of attention. So, imagine how heavy another's displeasure is to them. Tigger falls hard when all his efforts to be liked come up empty. It is so painful to him when the only attention he receives is negative. This is especially important to consider when communicating with a little Tigger. Young Tiggers will often misinterpret our displeasure with their actions, as a rejection of them. Without encouragement and being corrected with kindness in childhood, it can result in unhealthy Tiggers. By the way, this goes for Owl, Piglet and Rabbit, too.

Because of their core need for order and control, Owl and Rabbit will expect Piglet and Tigger to complete a task step-by-step or complete a project quickly in a particular way. What happens very often is that after Piglet and Tigger have completed the task or accomplished the project, Owl and Rabbit often point out what was done wrong or what should have been done quicker, while Piglet and Tigger focused on the team and just finishing the project. What is of major importance to one character is often of minor importance to another.

Connecting to the Source: More Than Appearances

"Train a child in the way they should go, and when they are old, they will not turn from it."
Proverbs 22:6

Proverbs 22:6 is a verse that is often misunderstood and not always interpreted correctly. I've heard many a prayer invoking this verse as some sort of insurance policy that if we raise our children in the church, then even though they may rebel against God, they will one day return to Him. Now that's a nice sentiment, but that's <u>not</u> what this verse says.

What this verse means is, "encourage a child in the way they are *bent.* In other words, cheer them on in what they lean toward, how they are gifted and what they excel at. Let's use a school report card as an example.

Your child Anna has come home from school with a report card hidden deep within a backpack, because she got a poor grade in math. However, her art, dance and music scores were absolutely perfect. Her English, history and science grades were pretty good, too. So, when you ask Anna about her report card. She begins to fidget. Then to cry. You gently put your arm around her and ask, "Baby, what's wrong?" She begins to reply through her sobs that she is terrible at math, and she is a failure. *Now is Anna a failure?* No, she is not. Does she struggle with a particular subject? Yes, just like most of us, Anna is strong in some subjects while being weaker in others. But knowing that Anna loves music, dance and art, you look at her report card and celebrate those areas where she is excelling in first. She has A's in music, art and dance! You remind Anna that she is not a failure and offer to spend time with her in math homework. Cheer her on in what she is leaning towards. And at the same time, give her tools to do her best in places where she struggles, so she can overcome her fear of failure. That is part of the "training up" parents are to do.

Gondola Stop #6

Everyone knows some part of Samson's story. He was strong because his hair was never cut. Until one day, it got cut by his enemies. They seized him, gouged out his eyes and bound him in bronze shackles. In the end, while bound to the temple pillars, he prays for God to enable his strength one final time, so that he could bring the temple down on his enemies' heads and his own. He died in honor and is spoken of in the Hall of Faith in Hebrews 11.

But before all of that, Samson, who was very much a Tigger, was blessed by God and stirred by the Spirit of the Lord. Before he was even born, an angel told his mom about him—told her he would be a Nazarite (no strong drink and no cutting his hair) from the womb until his death. The same angel of the LORD also visited his dad and instructed him regarding his son. They gave a burnt offering to honor the LORD. So, Samson was born into a wonderful calling. This strong man loved to use riddles to stump folks with his challenges—and he did so with flair. He also had a penchant for the wrong sort of woman. It would be his undoing—ending in his death. Yet, God had a purpose for his life—to break the yoke of control that the Philistines had on the Israelites. And so, he fulfilled that calling in the end. Samson's timeline was shortened earlier, perhaps, but it was an important blip in the Bigger Story. His would be a lasting testimony of the greatness of God, working through a man.

Chapter Seven: In Which We Process the Processing Process

"What day is it?" asked Pooh.
"It's today," squeaked Piglet.
"My favorite day," said Pooh."

A.A. Milne

Every personality or character is equally valuable and important. In order to lead a balanced or healthy life, it will require that we function in at least some measure of **all four core needs**... or at the very least, respect the core needs of others. So why is there so much conflict and misunderstanding between the characters?

I'm glad you asked.

Imagine that all four characters are sitting around a small table. In the center of the table is an empty 8 oz. plastic water bottle. Next to it is a measuring cup with 8 oz. of clear water.

From where they are seated Owl, Piglet, Rabbit and Tigger can clearly see and agree that there is a plastic water bottle and a measuring cup of water next to it. Owl might be wondering if there's exactly 8 oz. of water, while Piglet (*who is very thirsty*) would never ask to drink the water... besides Rabbit or Tigger would beat them to it. Everyone agrees so far, but conflicts and issues are about to arise.

Now imagine that the plastic water bottle is the lens through which you view life and other people and that the water represents the conflicts or issues you have with others. As long as the bottle and water are still on the table, the conflicts and issues can be easily dealt with, but rarely in conflict is that the case.

Still using our imaginations, take the 8 oz. cup of water and pour it into the water bottle and cap it. It's still a water bottle, and the only difference is that there's water in it now. Everyone still agrees. However, in life and especially in conflict, most of us tend to take the bottle from the table and hold it directly in front of our eyes. By doing this our view becomes distorted. Instead of still being able to see the others seated at the table and the water bottle on the table, this simple "change in perspective" intensifies the conflicts and issues. Why? Because instead of looking **at** the issue, we tend to look **through** the issue and so everywhere we look and everyone we see (through the water bottle) is the issue, except us of course.

Looking through the water bottle obscures our vision. We become short-sighted. After years of working with couples, families and businesses to resolve issues, I've discovered that most of their problems are a result of each of them looking through the issue, not at it, and the difference in the way they process what they see.

There are two basic ways in which our four characters process, but there are four different reasons why. Unless you know them well, you might confuse an Owl for a Piglet, because they process similarly--just as Rabbit and Tigger process similarly, but their reasoning is what determines which character they are. To fully grasp how each character processes, it's helpful to know how each character relates to others as well. Not knowing how each of the four characters (generally) interacts with others often leads to frustration, misunderstandings and hurt feelings.

Here's a snapshot of how each one processes and interacts with others.

Owl: Slow processor and cool or standoffish toward other people
Piglet: Slow processor and warm or accommodating toward other people
Rabbit: Quick processor and cool or intolerant toward other people
Tigger: Quick processor and warm or engaging toward other people

Owl and Piglet process most decisions **slowly**, while Rabbit and Tigger process most decisions **quickly**. Take note of the word "most." You may have noticed that using words like "always" and "never" has been avoided, as much as possible. Using absolutes when dealing with people and personalities invites trouble. *Owls are unique from other Owls,* and *Piglets are unique from other Piglets.* So, each will process at different rates depending upon the type of decision. If you ask Owl what "7 times 7" is, there's no hesitation in answering, "49!" But if you ask Owl a question that they don't **already** know the answer to, sit back, have a cup of coffee and you'll get the correct answer... eventually.

It would not be wise to assume that each character's behavior is based solely upon their main core need. However, when a character type can only function within the borders of a singular core need, it can reveal a lot about their mental or emotional health. When healthy, all of the characters desire all of the other core needs, but at various times and at different levels. So, depending on how you value the other core needs in relation to your core need (as well as taking into consideration what your family dynamics and environments contribute when you were growing up) is what creates the uniqueness of a Piglet among Piglets.

Not to muddy the water... each character type even has a unique ***"Love Language," but that's a whole other book that I highly recommend (see Appendix B).

OWL
Likes: Order
Needs to Work on: Mercy
Process: ...oh, alright

RABBIT
Likes: Control
Needs to Work on: Trust
Process: They're in my way

PIGLET
Likes: Harmony
Needs to Work on: Speaking the Truth
Process: They need me

TIGGER
Likes: Fun
Needs to Work on: Discipline
Process: Party!

The Research Project

In order to make a decision, both Owl and Piglet need T-I-M-E. By the way, just because they process slowly is not an indictment on their intellect. Some of the best chemical/mechanical engineers are Owls, and Piglets make great pharmacists. Though they both process slowly, their reason for doing so is what determines whether they are an Owl or a Piglet. Let's take a closer look at Owl.

Owl needs time to make a decision systematically, analytically and in an orderly fashion. Owl doesn't rely on or employ their emotions in the process, as emotions are not *always* based on facts, they are usually based on feelings. Feelings, no matter how real and sincere, can come as a result of bad information. Owl has no time for emotion, which gives him a reputation for being aloof or socially awkward.

Owl is rarely tempted to speed up the process by cutting corners or skipping a step. If another team member is tasked to do research, Owls have a tendency to **re**-research the research that someone else already did. This "double-checking" is common among Owls, and this seemingly small and insignificant act of "just making sure" can have unintended negative consequences in Owl's relationships with coworkers, as well as with his family and friends.

In his mind, Owl just wants to *"make sure that he is sure of the surety"* of the information he received from someone else. When it's discovered by the coworker, who did the same research, she might wonder why she wasted her time doing the research, if Owl is going to do it anyway! She then might assume that Owl doesn't trust her, that Owl is skeptical of her intelligence or not confident in her ability to properly do research. What often results is that people, who sit only a few feet apart geographically, separated by a wall or partition, are miles and miles apart in how they interpreted what just transpired between them.

After Owl received the research from a coworker, and then did his own research, his thinking typically is like this:

Owl: *"Now that I'm sure of all the information, I can make my decision."*

When the group discovers that Owl did the same research that they were assigned to do, the other characters' thinking typically is like this:

Piglet: *"What did I do wrong?"*
Rabbit: *"What's their problem? I just wasted six hours of time doing unnecessary research!"*
Tigger: *"They don't like me."*

I've seen this type of scenario played out countless times between coworkers and family members. Our core need drives us, while driving others crazy. Yes, there are unhealthy versions of each character; and granted, there are a few Owls on the planet who seem to enjoy driving others nutty, but for the most part Owls are seeking to have an orderly life. In their search for order, they can unintentionally send the wrong message to others. What helps in situations like these is to have a conversation between Owl and the person who the research was delegated to. And remember that it's a **conver**sation not an **accu**sation that helps.

No matter the character type, no one likes the feeling of being accused. When we feel accused, our natural instinct to is to become defensive. And depending on our personality-type, it determines how we defend ourselves.

Here's some very broad and generalized examples of what we use in our defense.

Owls: Refer to their facts and lean into the conflict.
Piglets: Defers to their intent and hopes to tamp down any further conflict.
Rabbits: Assert their authority and decide there will be no further conflict.
Tiggers: Do whatever it takes to rid themselves of a negative assessment and avoid further conflict.

For the sake of argument, let's give Owl the benefit of the doubt on the research issue and believe that Owl had no ulterior motive for doing the research that was delegated to Piglet, Rabbit, or Tigger. Any of the three responses listed above would be a total surprise to Owl. *Why?* Because Owl most likely didn't attach any emotion to his decision to research the research, he just wanted to be sure that they were sure.

If Piglet finds his courage, he will typically send an email asking Owl, *"What did I do wrong?"* Rabbit will likely walk right into Owl's office, lean over the desk and demand, *"What's your problem? I just wasted six hours of my time doing unnecessary research!"* And Tigger will most likely stew in his office, telling another coworker what Owl did. Owl may not have a clue what Piglet and Rabbit are referring to and certainly has no clue that Tigger is moping and commiserating in his office. Once again, Owl needs T-I-M-E to process the email from Piglet, the confrontation with Rabbit, and way more time to figure out why Tigger is avoiding him and why others in the office stop talking when Owl enters the room.

Here are Five Signs You Need to Know Yourself and Others Better

1. When something needs repair, do you just stop using it or turn it around, so it looks okay?
2. Have you ever reloaded the dishwasher just to prove that you can get more in it?
3. Does a missing disc from your *Lord of the Rings* DVD collection drive you crazy?
4. While waiting in line in the express lane with your one item, do you find it difficult to ask the person in front of you (who's cart is overflowing) if you can go ahead of them?
5. When playing a new game do you start playing and then learn the rules along the way?

Re-Mowing the Lawn

A few years ago, a young man that I'd known for several years asked to meet with me. As he shared what was going on in his life, he recounted a time from his teenage years when he mowed the lawn for his father. He took his time mowing the yard, mowing the way that his father had requested. Pleased with his work, he went inside to clean up. When he got out of the shower, he thought he heard a lawnmower running.

Peering out his bedroom window, he looked down to see that his father was mowing the lawn all over again. As he relived this experience, he broke down into tears, as he recalled standing at the window, wrapped only in a towel screaming at his father at the top of his lungs, *"What's wrong with me? Why are you doing that? I hate you!"* What began as questions, devolved into a declaration of hate. As he and I discussed further, he discovered that his hatred was not really toward his dad but was directed at himself. I'm guessing that I don't need to tell you who the Owl and who the Piglet were in this scenario.

People Principles

The reason that Owl appears cool or standoffish toward people is rather simple. If Owl is going to take T-I-M-E to process a purchase, then it stands to reason that he will also need T-I-M-E to process a person. Owls are cool toward people that he doesn't know and is even cooler toward people that he doesn’t trust. Before Owl will invest his hard-earned money into a house, car or coffee maker, he takes time to do the research, so it makes sense that Owl will take the time needed to research before investing his time and energy into a person.

So, don’t get frustrated that it takes a while for an Owl to warm up to a stranger and even longer for someone they don’t trust... and still longer to warm to a Tigger. Owls are predisposed to being especially cool toward Tiggers. Tiggers are almost completely the opposite of Owls, and they tend to violate all of Owls rules. Ironically... Owls tend to marry Tiggers and Tiggers tend to marry Owls. *Why?* Well, every kite needs a string, and every string needs a kite. Owls keep Tiggers from flying to close to the sun and getting tangled up in the trees. And Tiggers help Owls to get off the ground and spread their wings because after all, Owls were made to fly.

Because of some subtleties, it can be hard to tell the difference between Owl and Piglet. On the surface they both follow the rules and want to do the right thing. Below the surface Owl has an expectation that others do as Owl does, while Piglet has no expectation of others to do as they do. Piglets often allow others to behave in ways that they would never allow themselves to do.

Piglets’ need for T-I-M-E in processing has to do with their need to make sure their choice or decision is okay with (or doesn't inconvenience) everyone else. Piglets’ natural tendency to be aware of others' needs is thoughtful, even commendable, but when that thoughtfulness and "others-awareness" becomes unhealthy, Piglets become "others-focused" (We'll learn more about awareness & focus in the next chapter).

Without meaning to, Piglets' inability to make up their mind will quickly frustrate the Rabbits and Tiggers in their life, so what often occurs is that Rabbit or Tigger will decide for them... and given enough time, even an Owl will decide for a Piglet. By the way... an Owl rarely if ever lets another person make a decision for them.

So how can you tell if you're dealing with an Owl or A Piglet when making a decision? First you must remember the reason why they are slow processors. Owl wants to get it right; Piglet wants it to be okay.

Piglets and Tiggers

Remembering that Piglets and Tiggers are both warm toward people sometimes makes for an "I'm nicer than you are contest." Piglets defer to others, while Tiggers like to be liked, so decisions and choices can turn into a standoff.

Both tend to procrastinate or avoid issues and decisions, as Piglets want to make sure that what they do or choose is okay with others, while Tiggers procrastinate or avoid because doing things like chores, paying bills or writing reports is not much fun and so they get put off until the last minute. This "avoiding or putting things off" would drive a Rabbit, and especially an Owl, crazy, but Tiggers often thrive under pressure. They tend not to plan things out in steps, but rather dump the truck, and do all that falls out at the same time.

Piglets often do *make plans* but will defer to other's plans. They avoid delivering bad news, but don't typically put off doing chores, paying bills or writing reports... unless they're in a relationship with a Tigger. Let me tell you about Tammy and Marcus.

Tammy's whirlwind of activity and spending time with her is always an "adventure of the unexpected." She is fast paced, her plans turn on a dime, and she exudes energy. In other words, Tammy is a Tigger. True story: we once had a pendulum wall clock that had a dead battery and when Tammy walked past it, the pendulum began swinging back and forth for a day and a half after her visit... I swear!

Yes, Tammy is a lot of fun and a classic avoider of things that *aren't fun*. She's married to Marcus, who is a Piglet. Marcus does most of the chores, pays the bills and his job requires him to write reports... lots of them. They are a loving couple and make others feel wonderful when they are in their company. But they, like all couples, have issues in their relationship. The main source of conflict in their marriage was money.

Tammy likes to spend money, and Marcus pays the bills. Tammy loves a good deal, and Marcus pays the bills. Tammy will see something on sale that is 50% off and purchase it with the idea that she just saved $250, when in fact she just spent $250… and Marcus pays the bills. Because Marcus loves Tammy and avoids conflict, when Tammy calls him from the store telling him about the 50% off deal, instead of saying, "we don't have the money for that right now," Marcus capitulates and mumbles a less than enthusiastic "Mmm-mm," giving Tammy the green light for the purchase.

There are two things at play with this money issue, and both personalities are responsible for the problem. First let's look at Tammy because Marcus is a little more complex.

Tammy, being a Tigger, is on the prowl for fun and adventure. She sees something that she wants but doesn't need and because it's 50% off… *now* is the time to buy it… *right now*. She doesn't consider what she's paying as having the greater impact on their finances, but what they are saving. It's Tigger's impulsivity that spends to save, it's just that simple.

When Marcus, being a Piglet, wants peace and harmony and hears how excited Tammy is on the phone, he just can't bring himself to say "no" to her request. All the while, knowing full well that they don't have the money for it, Marcus gives Tammy permission to put in on their credit card. It's Piglet's passivity that gives into spending the $250, but there's a little more to this.

On the outside this may look to some that Marcus is just being sweet to Tammy, but to others it might appear that he's a weakling. *Which is it?* Well, it could be both... or it might be neither. Perhaps it's something else altogether that few pick up on... selfishness. What? Hold the phone... that's not how Piglet's behave. Sure, they do—everyone, no matter their personality, has to battle selfishness. Piglet's is just a little more acceptable because it tends to look good on the outside.

Tammy and Marcus have an agreement that if either one of them spends more than $150 on anything, they have to have each other's permission. So, when Tammy called to get permission to spend the $250, Marcus didn't want to get into an argument about finances or have to deal with Tammy's disappointment (or frustration) if he said "no." So, Marcus chose to keep the peace and let her buy what she wanted. In this particular circumstance, Marcus wasn't being sweet or weak, he was simply being selfish. I know that sounds a bit harsh, understand that he didn't want to deal with a potential conflict, he didn't want Tammy to get mad, he didn't want anything to interfere with the current peace and harmony they were experiencing, so he just said "yes" and went about the rest of his day in peace. However, when you tamp down issues to "keep the peace," you never really get to "making or creating peace."

When the credit card bill came in the mail, the back of Marcus' neck felt warm as he looked at the new balance. His stomach turned when he saw the minimum payment due and then he looked at the ottoman that Tammy "just had to have," and he wanted to kick it. In the very short amount of time it took for him to go to the mailbox and return to the kitchen, Marcus' mood was altered from peaceful to uneasiness. Unbeknownst to Tammy, while stewing over the bill, Marcus began internally building his case against Tammy's over-spending and it was going to stop… today.

As Marcus was putting the final touches of his case together, everything wrong pointed to Tammy. She's impulsive, she's not the one who pays the bills, she's all about stuff and she doesn't even know how much money we have in the bank. Well yeah… but Marcus does know that Tammy can be impulsive, he knows that he pays the bills, Marcus is all about different kinds of stuff than Tammy, and HE KNOWS HOW MUCH MONEY IS IN THE BANK. It's a little late to start blaming Tigger for the credit card bill, maybe if a few weeks earlier Piglet had been willing to sacrifice some "peace in the moment" for some longer lasting peace, the issue would be a non-issue.

What could have gone differently? First, if Tammy understood her Tigger traits better and that she tends to be impulsive, she could have self-regulated her desires and actions and probably could have passed on the 50% off sale. However, since Tammy and Marcus had not yet taken the *Who the Pooh are You?* (WTPAY) assessment (See Appendix A), we had to work with what we had. When Tammy called Marcus about saving $250, since Marcus pays the bills and he knows how much money is in the bank, he could have told Tammy right then and there that even though he wished she could get what she wanted... they couldn't afford to spend $250 on an ottoman. And there was one more element to this conflict that needed to be revealed.

Remember what Marcus did when he saw the credit card bill? Yes, the back of his neck got warm, but that's not what I was going for. He started to internally build a case against Tammy's spending and when he did this, he assumed how she would react and how she would respond. He was certain as to how the entire conversation between them would go... in his mind of course. He prepared his points in anticipation of how he "knew" what she would say. Apparently, Tammy didn't even need to be present because he already knew what's going to happen and maybe he won't bring it up after all. But he did, and that's why they were in my office.

What Marcus did when he saw the bill was exactly what he did when Tammy called about the ottoman. Instead of talking to Tammy, he talked to himself and created an internal conversation as to how Tammy would react and respond if he said "no," and he just didn't want to deal with it. This decision was not only selfish (to keep the peace), but disrespectful to Tammy. Not only did he not give her the benefit of the doubt (*that she might not have reacted the way he had assumed*), but that he never told her about the lack of funds. If he had, she could have been the one to make the wise choice. How do I know this? I'm glad you asked...

While Tammy and Marcus were telling their story, what I noticed was that they both had a habit of anticipating what the other would say or do... in other words, they assumed that they could read each other's minds. Both of them utilized internal conversations, so *real conversations between them* had become anemic and atrophied.

In Which, Money Matters

Each of the four characters approach people, problems, relationships and decisions differently, so it's no surprise that a very important part of life would be approached differently too.
Remembering what each character needs or seeks, it's kind of easy to figure out how they deal with their finances. Let's start with a simplified view of how each character spends and saves their money.

Owl needs order/rules and seeks security (for themselves and family) so they tend (after much consideration/research) to spend reluctantly because they are concerned about their future and the future of their loved ones. Owls don't always live in the moment but are concerned about the coming times ahead, so they save enthusiastically for retirement and cautiously invest in low-risk ventures.

Piglet needs harmony/peace and seeks safety (for themselves and others) so they tend to spend thoughtfully and enthusiastically to share with others. Piglets tend to support multiple charities and are an easy mark for their friends who need gas money or "forgot their wallet" when dining out. Piglets understand the value of money, but don't feel compelled to save for savings' sake. They will save for their future, but always considerate of others who may need a loan or a free meal.

Rabbit needs control/competency and seeks self-worth and will spend enthusiastically not only because they like having the biggest, brightest and best of everything, but because Rabbits know that they can always go make more money. More grandiose than and Owl, Rabbits save by growing their money by reinvesting it. Unlike Owl, Rabbits have no fear of investing in high-risk ventures because high risk often leads to high reward.

Tigger needs attention/approval and because they love being special, they spend enthusiastically on themselves and others. Tiggers often hold to the idea that if there's still checks in their checkbook or have a credit card in their pocket, there's an endless supply of funding available to them. Tiggers have a very bad habit of spending the same money twice... thrice... you get the idea. For Tiggers, "save" is a four-letter word and since they live mostly in the moment, they typically take no thought of retirement, they think a 401K is the latest version of X-box.

Connecting to the Source: Making Offerings Not Demands

When it comes to our personalities, "if we don't own it, we can't export it." In other words, if we don't possess (within ourselves) the qualities that we desire in others, we are creating a sort of Ponzi scheme. In other words, we can't truly export it, if we project it. And we can't with any authenticity or integrity bring what we are supposed to bring if we're always trying to project it rather than export it. We have to own it first. So, we carry within us harmony. We carry within us self-control. We carry within us a sense of order and a sense of acceptance. So, if we don't truly own it, we cannot export it. We were simply projecting it all the while. It was pretending at its finest.

We are to offer gifts; we don't demand that others receive them. So, when giving a gift, we are thinking of what the recipient needs/wants rather than *our wants*. In the book of First Corinthians, chapter 14, it says that when we assemble together that everyone should bring something to build others up. We can bring with us harmony. We can bring self-control. We can bring within us a sense of order. We can bring with us a sense of acceptance. For you see, we were created to share our gifts and share what's been given to us for the benefit of others and community, not thinking of ourselves as more important than anyone else, but rather that to serve those that we live with, work with and love.

Hebrews 10:24-25a says it this way, *"And let us consider how we may spur one another on toward love and good deeds. Let us not give up meeting together, as some are in the habit of doing, but let us encourage one another..."*

Gondola Stop #7

So far from our gondola journey, we have seen some wonderful people in the Bible with wonderful callings, but I want to stop the gondola mid-air right now.

I hope the rocking doesn't scare you too much. *Yes, the wind can be fierce up here! Do you see storm clouds in the distance? Yeah, isn't that amazing? Oh, you saw lightning, too? It's okay, we are secure on this particular gondola ride, because #1) it's in your imagination and #2) you are in God's hands, no matter what you do or where you go. He's here right now.*

The fact is God planned in advance for this ride. He planned in advance that you would read this book. And right now, *lean in close to hear me*, **He has an irrevocable calling on your life**. That means no matter who you are, where you've been, what you've done, who you have hung around or even what drives your thoughts and actions right now...the God of all creation, LORD of all, has come near to tell you that He not only placed the giftings in your life, your personality and even the circumstances surrounding all that I mentioned, He still has a calling on your life that He wants to come alongside to help you fulfill. That calling matters in the Bigger Story. It matters *more than you will ever know* this side of Heaven.

Do you ever think any of the people in the Bible, besides Jesus, knew that we'd still be talking about them today? Joseph, the carpenter, or Joseph, the favorite son with the colorful coat – both with masterful God-stories over their lives. One would die fairly young, but he would raise the Son of God. *Stop and think about that for a moment.* He would be training up God's Son in the way he should go. He would be wiping Jesus' tears and listening to his chatter about what the kids said today. He would tell dad jokes that made Jesus laugh 'til he couldn't breathe. The other Joseph would be given the gift of imprisonment and of being hated by most of his brothers. And God would use that imprisonment to save the lives of ALL his family and of Egypt and of nations surrounding Egypt. He would be blessed to ***SEE his dreams come to***

fruition...and that fruition came through quite a bit of pain, sorrow and anguish of spirit that stayed long with him.

So, two regular, average Josephs...one regular, average *you*.... All called with irrevocable callings—to be and to do that which God Himself planned in advance for you to do. Perhaps you feel even less than average and could tell me why, while we are stopped here a moment. *Mmm, hmm. Yes. I'm listening. I hear you.*

Okay, are you ready to hear the most wonderful news? God likes to confound the wisdom of the wise, and He actually uses the average ones to do just that. *OH YEAH!* He likes a good plot twist. But even more so, you have His Spirit in you, as you believe on His Son Jesus, to give you **EXACTLY** what you need to accomplish anything He has called you to do.

"His divine power has given you EVERYTHING you need—for life and godliness, through the knowledge of Christ, who calls you by His own GLORY and His GOODNESS"
(2 Peter 1:3 NIV).

Now isn't that something? Let's move on again. Yes, looks like the storms have passed us now!

A quick summary so far...
If you need financial advice or discerning what the right thing to do is, OWL is the wise choice.

If you need compassion or someone to listen empathetically to your problems, PIGLET is safe.

If you're having trouble with motivation or completing a project, RABBIT will get'r done.

And if you need encouragement or just want to have fun, TIGGER is who you want bouncing around.

Chapter Eight: In Which We Focus on the Focus

"You can't stay in your corner of the Forest waiting for others to come to you.
You have to go to them sometimes."

A.A. Milne

Aware of Your Focus

As we have discovered thus far, each of the four characters has one of four distinctive core needs and each character displays distinctive behaviors and characteristics, but with a few common traits i.e. how they process (slowly vs. quickly) or relate to others (warmly vs coolly).

Short of sounding like I'm psychoanalyzing or delving too deep, I'd like to introduce another grouping of four behaviors that deal with how Owl, Piglet, Rabbit and Tigger manifest their core need when interacting with other people. It's an attempt to peer through their eyes and discover how they "see the world" or to more clearly state it, to discover how they view themselves in relation to how they view others.

This may also help you to recognize why in some social settings that you are quickly "put off" by certain people and not others. These four behaviors are:

Self-focused
Others-focused
Self-aware
Others-aware

Self-focused

> [Please remember that I'm not a psychologist and please also note that the self-focused behavior I'm referring to is not to be confused with "Self-focused Attention" which is common in several emotional disorders. Self-focused Attention related to social phobia and social anxiety is a serious condition that requires professional intervention, and a list of helpful resources are included at the back of the book. (Clinical Psychology Review Vol 22 Issue 7 September 2002 Jane M Spurr/Luisa Stopa)
>
> This is just a simple 30,000 ft. view of the self-focused behaviors associated with our lovable characters Owl, Piglet, Rabbit and Tigger.]

The very fact that Owl has even shown up at a party or social event is cause for celebration. Owls are not (by nature) social creatures. They like to stick to their routines, and they like their ruts long and deep. Self-focused Owls would be overjoyed if all parties and social gatherings were outlawed... unless they were hosted by them of course. Both Owl and Rabbit are cool toward people, but unlike Rabbit, Owl's adherence to the rules of proper etiquette keep them a little quieter... that is until they see someone they know or until they get to know someone at the party. Only then will an Owl start talking... and what a self-focused Owl does is *criticize*. A self-focused Owl talks about how the party inconvenienced him or interfered with his previous plans for the evening. He will talk about the ways the party should have been done differently and how he would have done it. He talks about what a loudmouth Rabbit is and that the Tigger over there is such a big phony. Being self-focused clouds Owl's objectivity from acknowledging that other people may have also changed their plans to be at the party, that others have routines and schedules to keep. That's why Owls come across as judgmental, petty, and nit-picky.

Somewhere at the party may be lurking a self-focused Piglet. They, like Tigger, are quite charming and warm to people. While a Tigger will hold others hostage energetically, endlessly talking about nothing, a Piglet will listen with rapt attention to someone's boring story (that they've already heard many times before) adding ooh's and ah's, as encouragement. (It could be said that Piglets have the ability to listen to someone talk about absolutely nothing and take notes).

To spot a self-focused Piglet, your best bet is to head toward the kitchen and look to see who is cleaning up or refilling drinks and replenishing the food trays... but... wait for it... they aren't the host of the party. Self-focused Piglets have a need to feel needed and indispensable and that without their help the host couldn't get through this party. So how is Piglet's helpfulness being self-focused? *Because you're seeing them doing it aren't you?* It would be one thing if Piglet's help went unnoticed, but a self-focused Piglet needs to be needed is equal to his need to be seen being needed. His serving tends toward his being "underfoot" and his intent to be helpful can become a nuisance. Piglet takes on the suffering-servant role, and like Tigger, they can unintentionally be deceptively manipulative. If they love serving and helping... why do they complain about not being appreciated later? That's why self-focused Piglets can come across as overly helpful, needy and even pushy.

Though all four personalities can be self-focused, its fairly easy to quickly spot a self-focused Rabbit or Tigger at a party or social gathering. You don't even have to see them because to know that they're there... you can hear them even before you enter the room. They're the ones that are usually doing most of the talking... which is usually about themselves... and they never seem to stop for air. They tend to be oblivious of the feelings of others, and they can project the impression that they are the most important or intriguing people in the room–everyone else is an audience.

A self-focused Rabbit will talk and laugh louder than everyone else, and he will consistently talk over or interrupt others. When someone else is telling a story that is similar to one of Rabbit's experiences, Rabbit will shanghai the story already in progress and proceed with telling his story–all while being completely unaware that other people are cringing with social anxiety. Being self-focused clouds a Rabbit's objectivity on what is interesting, funny or even appropriate in conversations with others, and that's why he can come off as crass, boorish or oafish. Sadly, even though everyone else has known it for hours, self-focused Rabbits tend to quickly wear out their welcome at social gatherings long before they (if ever) realize it.

A few nuances separate a self-focused Tigger and a self-focused Rabbit. They both tend to be loud and interruptive, but Tigger tends to be a little more tolerable and appears to be less arrogant. Because Tigger is much more polished and charming, which unbeknownst to others (and Tigger themselves), he can be deceptively manipulative. Rabbits tend to be cool toward people and don't much care if you like them, so they are just who they are and tell their stories (sometimes with exaggeration) with them as the main character or victor. Tiggers are warm to people and have a higher emotional I.Q. than most Rabbits, so they tend to adapt their personalities and exaggerate their stories to suit and please others. Insecurity often clouds Tiggers' objectivity, so they try harder and harder to woo and entertain at the party and that's why they get a reputation for being insincere, spastic or childish.

In summary, Rabbit's goal is to impress and get everyone focused on him and listening to his stories, while Tigger's goal is to entertain and get everyone focused on him, so that they will like him more than anyone else, including Rabbit. Tiggers are also usually the last to leave. It's not as easy to quickly spot a self-focused Owl or Piglet because they don't initially stand out. Owl's goal is to avoid conversations with people he doesn't know, and be the first to leave, while Piglet's goal is to ensure that before he leaves, everything is all cleaned up. He will even offer to stay later if need be.

If reading about these behaviors makes you feel uncomfortable or defensive, then you may have some homework to do. Remember that we are talking about self-focused versions of Owl, Piglet Rabbit and Tigger. When people are made aware of their unhealthy behaviors, they often desire to change them. But they can only change them if they decide to. Desiring and deciding are two different things. I can desire to lose weight, but unless I decide to stop eating ice cream every night, my desire to fit into my new suit will never come to fruition. There's more about this in upcoming chapters, so don't skip ahead Rabbit and Tigger... *I know you're already distracted but hang in there!*

Others-focused

All four characters have a tendency to be self-focused, but all four characters can and will display others-focused behavior...but for different reasons and in very different ways.

I personally don't know of anyone who enjoys being around a "self-focused" person for very long. *Why?* Because everything and anything is all about them... all for them... and all the time. So, does it stand to reason that being with an "others-focused" person would be more enjoyable? Actually, no. Why? Because everything and anything is never ever about them at any time. And similar to being with a "self-focused" person... when you are with an "others-focused" person, instead of two people spending time together, it can feel like there's only one person in the room. When you're with a "self-focused" person, it's just them, their decisions and their opinions. When you're with an "others-focused" person, it's just you, your decisions and your opinions. Something to note... there is a very thin line between being self-focused and others-focused. You'll see what I'm talking about...

We used a social setting for self-focused behaviors, so we'll use a workplace setting for others-focused behaviors. There is a problem with a major client and all four characters are called, one by one, into a meeting with upper management to account for why his department is responsible for the problem with the Meyers project.

Owl arrives at the meeting ten minutes early with folders, binders, graphs, email transcripts. He waits somewhat patiently for management to arrive. After management reads the client's complaint, Owl methodically uses the folders, binders, graphs and email transcripts to explain that, not only did he do everything correctly and "by the book," he also describes in great detail what each of the other three employees did wrong... including not listening to Owl's advice. Owl takes no responsibility in this matter, and even expects an apology from management, for the interruption of his day. This others-focused behavior clouds Owl's objectivity and causes him to have strained business (and personal) relationships. Since he is absolutely certain that he is right, this gives no margin or thought that when something goes awry, it could be because of Owl. It's always someone else. He prefers to work alone and document his work–and when others make mistakes–instead of helping them. He tends to document the others' mistakes and then later, if called upon to give an account, Owls are adept at "throwing others under a bus." That's why others-focused Owls come across as mean, dismissive and tattletales.

Rabbit will show up talking on a cellphone, just as the meeting starts. Still talking, he drops his briefcase or backpack on the conference table, while motioning to management with his index finger that it'll just be another minute. After he's certain that management has overheard how important Rabbit is to the Briggs' deal, he finally hangs up. Before management even finishes the complaint, Rabbit has taken over the meeting–even questioning management's decisions and personnel choices. Rabbit wasn't given the authority he needed from management, and because Rabbit is never wrong, the other three are the ones that screwed up the Meyers project. Being others-focused clouds a Rabbit's objectivity in taking responsibility for failure or mistakes. Because they are natural leaders and fixers, when failure occurs, Rabbits focus the blame on others. Others didn't do what Rabbit told them to do or listen to how Rabbit told them to do it. It's not Rabbit's fault; it's everyone else's. And whether he desires it or not, Rabbit will usually take credit for things that went right. This is why others-focused Rabbits come across as hard to work for, maniacal and ironically... egotistical.

Tigger? Um Tigger? If you wait long enough, Tigger will eventually show up at the meeting, but you might want to call or text to remind him that you're waiting. Though very much a people-pleaser, Tigger will most often be the tardiest of the four. It's not that he is being rude to management, it's that he was being others-focused toward the person he was meeting with prior to meeting with management. After sliding sideways into view of the doorframe (think Kramer from Seinfeld), Tigger breathlessly enters the conference room profusely apologetic for being late. Having forgotten his paperwork, he offers to run back to his office and get it, but management knows that "a Tigger in the room beats one in the hallway, where there are other conversations to be had." Tigger nods in full agreement, as the client's complaint is read. Management then recounts Owl's take of the situation, as Tigger enthusiastically nods. When Rabbit's side of the issue is brought to light, management is perplexed to see Tigger nodding in full agreement with the conflicting information. Others-focused Tiggers don't want any enemies, especially if they are in the same room. Tigger's nodding in agreement has less to do with the statements being read, but how management views him. Tigger agrees with management that the customer is always right, but who is responsible for the problem? Tigger doesn't want to say anything, but someone is at fault... but it most certainly isn't Tigger. Heck... Tigger isn't even sure that he is even on the Meyers' project. Since management's in the room, it can't be their fault; so, it must be someone who is not currently in the room. Because of their ability to "emotionally scan" a room, others-focused Tiggers will side with management's take on who is responsible and then leave the meeting quickly, if they suspect that management wants them to deliver the news to the responsible party. Being others-focused clouds a Tigger's objectivity, which makes it almost impossible to make an honest or critical assessment of another person's job performance that is in his presence. Tigger will equivocate and dodge direct confrontation and communication but will often share with other employees. That's why others-focused Tiggers come across as dishonest, backstabbing and untrustworthy.

Of all the characters, Piglet is the most natural at being others-focused. Even their self-focused behavior appears to be others-focused. So as to not keep management waiting, Piglet typically shows up to the meeting on time... unless, of course, someone else in the office needed something. In advance of the meeting, an others-focused Piglet may preemptively take everyone's coffee order and bring along homemade treats to the meeting. He makes sure that everyone is okay, so that the meeting can proceed. Piglet emotionally empathizes with the client, as their complaint is read, and he feels a real sense of personal responsibility for the breakdown of the project. When Owl, Rabbit and Tigger's versions of what went wrong are shared, Piglet again emotionally empathizes with each one, but at differing levels—more so with Tigger and to a lesser degree with Owl and then lesser to Rabbit.

Owl: "I have things to do and places to be."

Rabbit: "I know the best way to do things and what's best for this person."

Tigger: "I want to be this person's favorite!"

Piglet: "Are they okay? Are they angry? Are they angry with me? How can I make then stop being angry?"

The healthiest way of communing with ourselves and with others is to be self-aware and aware of others. It's a balanced tension between recognizing that I have needs and so does everyone else or everyone else has needs and so do I, depending upon your point of view. Self-focused says, "The heck with everyone else!" Others-focused says, "The heck with me!" Neither of these is healthy.

Focus on your Awareness

The healthiest way of communing with ourselves and with others is to, first, be **self-aware** and secondly, **aware of others**. It's a balanced tension between recognizing that, "I have needs, and so does everyone else" or "Everyone else has needs and so do I," depending upon your point of view.

Earlier in the chapter, we revealed two of four behaviors that the personality-types display when interacting with others. The first two were unhealthy behaviors, self-focused and others-focused.

> In summary: Self-focused is basically, "The heck with everyone else, I'm going to get my needs met!" Others-focused is basically, "The heck with me, I'm going to meet everyone else's needs, even if that means that I don't meet the needs of my spouse and my children, as well."

If you're even remotely good at math and you haven't skipped ahead (Rabbit) or you are not watching television while you're reading this (Tigger), you know that there are only two behaviors remaining. *And Owl and Piglet know that both remaining behaviors are the healthy ones.*

They are as follows: self-aware and others-aware.

I'd like to write a lengthy, revelatory and awe-inspiring chapter on these two behaviors, but come on… is that really necessary?

Honestly… mostly no, *but with a little bit of yes.* **Being self-aware and others-aware is fairly self-explanatory and work best when they go hand in hand.**

Here are Five Signs You Need to Know Yourself and Others Better

1. When playing a new game, do you read all the rules prior to playing.
2. Have you ever loaded the dishwasher keeping sets together because they're like a little family of dishes?
3. If there is no line… are you good at making the cashier laugh and gladly welcome you and your overflowing shopping cart to the express lane?
4. When a disc is missing from the LOTR (Lord of the Rings) DVD collection, is it because you can't

remember where you put it as you were putting the next disc in the player?

5. When something needs repair, do you "fix it" quickly until you need to "fix it" again?

This Much

Debra and Jim were at a difficult place in their marriage. Over the last several years of building their family business and raising their two kids, Debra and Jim had stopped talking to each other, except for passing along cursory business information or their kids' sports activities and school schedules. They were cordial in public but would mostly grunt or grumble at each other at home. They had violated the "this much" principle that I teach to couples during pre-marital counseling sessions.

The "this much" principle is simple. I would demonstrate it by holding up my hands with my palms facing each other about an inch apart. I explained that due to a lack of trust (for real or perceived reasons), couples would not talk about "this much," which again was demonstrated by my hands being an inch apart. I explained that this seemingly little or insignificant amount of space was not so insignificant–as that little gap, when left unattended, would grow larger. My point was that when people in a relationship get comfortable not talking about "this much" (just an inch or so), it's not long before they become comfortable not talking about "this much," at which point I would demonstrate by increasing the separation between my hands by about six inches.

I continued to demonstrate the "this much" principle as each time I would say, "and when you're comfortable not talking about 'this much' you become comfortable with 'this much.'"

I would widen the gap between my hands with each successive level of "comfortable non-communication." Finally, when my hands were about two feet apart, I would simply say, "and when you're comfortable not talking about 'this much,' you're probably already talking to someone else that you'll never share (and closing the gap between my hands to about an inch again) 'this much' with either."

Outwardly, when being self and others-aware, it looks very much the same among all four personality-types with a few nuances and variations, but inwardly it is a whole different ball game. *Let's just say that there's a whole lot going on between the ears of our beloved critters.*

Chapter Nine: In Which We Go About Making Conclusions

"If the person you are talking to doesn't appear to be listening, be patient. It may simply be that he has a small piece of fluff in his ear."

A.A. Milne

Another difference in the way that personalities process is how they arrive at the final picture of how things should be. Owls tend to research and research all the information before coming to a conclusion, while Piglets, Tiggers and Rabbits see the final picture before they have all the information to back-up or prove their conclusions.

A Piglet intuitively, yet reservedly comes to a conclusion that is often mostly correct.

> An Owl methodically and slowly gathers information, so that he can be assured that everything is correct.

Piglets see the result before they have the information.

Owls can't come to a result until all the information is gathered.

Piglets gather people for consensus.

Owls gather information for consensus.

Can you see the potential conflicts when Piglet and Owl are asked to work on a project together?

A Tigger quickly, and with impulsive intuition, comes to a conclusion that is occasionally correct.

Owls employ method and procedure to come to a correct conclusion.

Tiggers skim whatever information or documentation they are given.

Owls intently read and will even make side notes of the information and documentation they received.

Tiggers will seek out others who agree with their conclusions.

Owls provide updates on what the research has revealed.

Can you feel the tempest brewing when Tigger and Owl work together?

Rabbits quickly see their version of the conclusion.

Owls slowly arrive at the correct conclusion.

Rabbits envision the results that they desire, information be damned.

Owls wait to see what the information will conclude.

Rabbits influence and direct others to agree with their conclusions.

Owls rely solely on what the information has revealed.

Because neither Rabbit nor Owl prefer to employ the assistance of others in this process, not everyone knows that a storm was brewing until it makes landfall.

So, what can we take away from this? Here's a simple outline to help deter unnecessary conflicts. Notice I used "unnecessary," as not all conflict is bad. In fact, when handled appropriately and with mutual respect, conflict can make each of us a better version of ourselves... but that's another chapter.

Give others room to make a decision or come to a conclusion.

Owls are uncomfortable going on record with a conclusion about something that they have no prior experience with or knowledge of until they do the research.

Piglets, even though they are certain that they are mostly correct, are not comfortable telling others their summation or conclusions until others have shared their conclusions.

Rabbits are comfortable telling others how they want and expect the end result to look.

Tiggers are comfortable telling others what they think the end result should look like, even though they just thought of it in that moment.

In Which, the SCENE Opens

Here's how a conversation might go if we were doing a scene from a movie.

Scene 1: BOARD ROOM

(Interior: Large office with large table and four chairs. PIGLET, OWL and RABBIT are already seated with their personal notebooks and papers laid on the table in front of them respectively. The door flies open and in rushes TIGGER finishing up a conversation on his cell phone. He takes the open seat and lays his cell phone on the table in front of him. There is already more than enough tension in the room without TIGGER adding to it by being late.)

RABBIT
(Addressing everyone)
So, where are we on the project?

PIGLET
(Timidly looking down at the notes in front of him)
Well, I know how the f-f-f-finished project is going to look, even though I don't have all the d-d-d-data or information compiled to prove it yet.

OWL
(Sternly looking at PIGLET)
How can you possibly know how it's going to look without all the data?

RABBIT
Excuse me, but all of you are aware of how I want it to look??

TIGGER
I just had an idea... I think it should look like this...

OWL
Ugh, Tigger... you don't even know what we're talking about and Rabbit, what if the data doesn't conclude that the way you see it, is correct or even possible?

PIGLET
(Nervously clearing his throat to get everyone's attention)
Alright everyone... let's all take a breath and hear what Tigger's idea is. After all, up until now he hasn't provided us with any research or information.

TIGGER
(Coyly smiling at PIGLET)
Not to be defensive Piglet, but neither have you.

RABBIT
(Standing up as if to leave)
Look, I don't have time to listen to you all argue about this, when can I expect delivery on this project?
OWL
Delivery? We haven't even started a cost or risk analysis, let alone received our demographic research report!

TIGGER
(Picking up his cell phone)

Oh yeah, I meant to send that demographic request last week, let me pull up my email to see if I still have that lady's contact info.

RABBIT
What? You don't even have that report in hand?
(Slowly sitting back down)

OWL
(Smiling, feeling vindicated)
You see Rabbit, this is what I've been trying to tell you, we don't have enough, (now specifically addressing Tigger)
if any information.

PIGLET
(Nervously shuffling papers in front of him)
Before you get mad at Tigger, I knew he was really busy, so I made the demographic study request, and I have the report here in my notes.

TIGGER
(Smiling at Piglet)
Thanks Piglet, I can always count on you to bail me out. By the way, can I borrow your car, mine's low on fuel.

OWL
(Now completely agitated)
Is there even an agenda for this meeting... or are we just wasting everyone's time?

FADE TO BLACK

I could have easily kept this dialogue going, but hopefully you got the gist. Each personality brings to the meeting their own particular intentions, along with their own unique way of processing. Also, it describes whether they need information and data before they can get to the final result (Owl) or they intuitively see the final picture before doing the research (Piglet) or they see what they want it to look like, research or not (Rabbit). And lastly, when called upon, in the moment can see the end result (Tigger).

In Which, We Wed

The personality traits bring their own issues into a marriage.

Piglets married to Piglets
Since Piglets are not big on conflict and others-oriented, disagreements don't often escalate and where they decide to go for dinner may fizzle out into staying home and eating frozen pizza.

Owls married to Owls
Since Owls are big on order, what they will most often butt heads about is whose order is best.

Rabbits married to Rabbits

Rabbits love control so their conflicts can get a little sporty and loud. It's not always determined by who wins as much, as it is which one gives up the fight first.

Tiggers married to Tiggers

Tiggers have a hard time keeping each other out of trouble. They both tend to spend money they don't have and seek out fun for fun's sake. Conflicts arise over who is in the spotlight and who spent money first, so that the other can't purchase what they wanted.

The Blame Game

Both Piglet and Tigger have a tendency toward "I heard."

Owl and Rabbit have a tendency to say, "you said."

When it comes to the ambiguity scale, Tiggers, then Piglets, then Rabbits have a tolerance for it. Owls have no tolerance for ambiguity.

When it comes to the importance of facts and figures scale it's Owl, Rabbit, Piglet, then Tigger.

Each character has a dominant or particular core need, but also has need for the other three, but in lesser and varying degree.

The dominant core need is revealed in times of stress and when everything seems to be going wrong. Owls will organize and straighten; Piglets will fret over relationships and apologize for things they didn't do. Rabbit will exert their authority and take over and Tigger will seek out friends, go shopping or both.

When Owls and Rabbits emote, they emote like Piglet or Tigger.

When Piglets and Tiggers act, they behave like Owl or Rabbit.

It's sometimes difficult to tell the difference between Owls and Rabbits, because order and control can mask each other. Remember that order is the "right way" to do it and control is "my way" of doing it.

Likewise, discerning between Piglets and Tiggers is tricky, because deferring Piglet's choice for the sake of harmony looks an awful lot like Tigger seeking acceptance. Piglet defers, so that "everyone is okay," and Tigger defers, so that "everyone likes me."

While observing someone learning to use a new app or program, as they follow procedures you might quickly assume they are an Owl, because they are "going by the book." But keep watching. How they respond when they find another or better way of doing the work that suits them is what determines whether they are an Owl or a Rabbit.

Owl will methodically follow the procedures, as written. If he finds another or better way of doing it that suits him, he will make a note of it and then keep following the procedures. He will check and recheck his work to make sure it's complete and then will ask permission to use his own procedures the next time he uses the program. Owl will send an email to follow up on his request with his new procedures written out in bullet points, in case you want everyone else to do it Owl's way too. But Rabbit will change procedures, as best suits him. If Owl does want to change the procedure, he will ask permission to do so.

Rabbit will follow the written procedures for a few minutes, but quickly finds shortcuts that suit him and will implement them immediately. He will sit at his desk and hammer away until the work is complete. While everyone else is still plodding through the new program, Rabbit will appear in your office doorway, state that some of the procedures are stupid and unnecessary and then tell you he did it his way, if you're smart, you'll have everyone else do it his way too.

While observing the same scenario above, it would be very easy to discern between a Piglet and a Tigger. While Piglet learns the program by following procedures, Tigger is playing solitaire... just kidding (sort of).

Piglet will sit quietly following the procedures, and if he finds another or better way of doing the work, he will either continue following procedures or change them (to suit himself), and then after the work is completed, he will apologize for doing it "his way." Or, if there are any mistakes, Piglet will offer to go back and do the same work all over again, using the written procedures if you want him to.

Tigger will do his best to follow procedures but will not sit quietly. He quickly finds an easier and faster way of doing the work, and now believing that since he can get the work done faster, he has time to bounce off to the break room for more coffee. Once there, Tigger forgets what he was working on and starts chatting it up with everyone in the break room. When Owl and Rabbit sees him in the break room, they ask Tigger if he finished his work. And because a Tigger "thinks it," he "did it." He'll reply with an emphatic, "You bet!" It's not until he bounces back to his office that he discovers that he really didn't finish. Then Tiggers begins working at a blazing speed, procedures be darned, to complete the work. If the work ever gets finished, he will apologize but be reluctant to assume responsibility for any mistakes.

"HOW DID YOU GET A "D" IN ALGEBRA?!"

How did you feel or how might your child feel with this statement?

Sadly, in a lot of households there is a focus and immediate reaction to the low grades. There could be five "A's" and one "D" and yet which grade gets all the attention? If your experience was like mine, it felt like the "D's" or low grade was the only grade on the report card. All those beautiful "A's" that you were so proud of were usually skipped right over without even an "attaboy" or "attagirl" and the interrogation commenced on why you have a "D" in the subject that you rationalized you'd never use in real life.

This is what **Proverbs 22:6** is all about. It's there to remind us to recognize, celebrate and applaud all those "A's". To take notice of and affirm what you or your child did well and then with some compassion... ask them about the low grade. When we start a conversation with what is "wrong" with someone else, it typically goes downhill from there. Having to give and answer or explain the "D" without any acknowledgement of our "A's" puts us all on the defensive and that's not best posture to take in any conversation.

What if the same report card received this response...?

"**Wow! 'Five A's'! That's amazing! I am so proud of you!"**
Already feels different, doesn't it?

No matter your personality-type (or Love Language) *, appreciation and encouragement are a great way to start any conversation... especially when the conversation is to challenge, get clarity on a behavior, instruct or bring correction. When the "A's" are acknowledged and celebrated there is a chemical released in our bodies called "oxytocin" or the "feel good hormone." Ironically and at the exact same time the person offering the praise or encouragement also receives a release of oxytocin to their system. Now that's a cool thing that God made too.

With the release of oxytocin, it's probably an opportune moment to inquire about the low grade. Instead of asking a derogatory question like, "What's wrong with you?" how about asking, "Can you tell about what's going on in algebra?" This gives the person the opportunity to explain rather than defend and is a conversation not a response to an accusation.

I found with my own children that if I purposely and honestly celebrated their good grades, I could eventually venture into a dialog about the low grades. One interesting note was that they each responded differently. For whatever reason I asked my children if they "liked" the teacher in the particular class they were struggling in. Not surprising, they both said, "no". But they had very different answers when I asked, "why?". One child said, "Because they don't like me." The other replied, "Because they're boring." It seems one of my children struggled because they were wounded while the other struggled because they were annoyed. *

Understanding Rabbits

For anyone familiar with Marvel Comics and the Avengers movie franchise, it is no secret that Iron Man, aka Tony Stark, is a Rabbit. Perfectly cast for the big screen role is Robert Downey Jr., who portrays an insatiable need for control, while at the same time revealing what can be endearing and charming about Rabbits. Tony Stark's need for control is common to a lot of Rabbits... they want control because they don't trust others to do what they want accomplished and the way they want it done. Some of the most entertaining scenes in the Avengers movies are when Tony Stark is in conflict with Dr. David Banner, Thor and especially Captain America. Stark will even verbally spar with Jarvis, who is an artificial intelligence computer program... that Stark created! Rabbits are natural born leaders and have a tendency to trust their own abilities over the ability of those they lead or are in relationships with. But sometimes their desire to control is accentuated, because of their past.

A good character always has a good story "arc." In other words, they have a past, present and future. To connect with or to care about a character in a book, play or movie, it's important for the audience to know what makes them tick. What makes the Marvel Movie franchise so successful is how each of the main characters, has a backstory. Black Widow was brainwashed, as a child, to be a Soviet spy and wants to "clear her ledger" of past sins. The Hulk is the unexpected result of experiments by Dr. David Banner, who wrestles to become whole again. Spiderman is a high school kid named Peter Parker, who is bitten by a radioactive spider. Peter's parents are dead, so he's being raised by his aunt and uncle until the day his beloved Uncle Ben was killed in a robbery gone awry. Peter blames himself for his uncle's death, and this event propels him to become a crime fighter. And then there is Iron Man.

What makes Iron Man so intriguing is the man inside the suit. Tony Stark is a study in complexity. He can at once be charming, magnanimous and captivating–and in an instant be rude, boorish and dismissive. Why? Because he has a past, he has a story. All Rabbits have a story... just as Owls, Piglets and Tiggers do.

Although a "Rabbit," there is also a "Tigger" component that resides in the Tony Stark's character. This can be somewhat confusing, depending upon the circumstances in which you encounter him. There is the fun-loving side of Tony Stark that is a risk taker, a partier and an unrepentant womanizer. If someone were to edit the Iron Man or The Avengers movies and only show you the scenes where he is at parties, drinking or giving witty speeches, the viewer might be of the opinion that Stark is a Tigger. But there is a whole movie to watch, and whenever his friends, fellow Avengers or innocents are in peril, Iron Man takes control of the situation and calls the shots.

Tony Stark is riddled with guilt from his past. Not only from his own behaviors and choices, but his father's as well. The genesis of Stark's impetus to fight crime and "do good" comes from the decisions his father made when he was developing and manufacturing weapons for the military. Tony Stark experiences what can happen when the weapons his father developed and produced end up in the wrong hands. Tony not only wants to right (what are in his view) the wrongs of his father's past, he also wants to atone for his own past sins. This "back story" helps the audience understand where a particular character is "coming from" and the "why" of their actions. When Tony Stark is being boorish, rude and dismissive toward another character, the audience has a "bird's eye view" of Stark's past and how it relates to motives and behavior. This understanding of his past allows the audience to give Stark the benefit of the doubt when he's apparently (from the other character's point of view) just being a jerk. Wouldn't it be great if life were like a movie? Maybe then, when someone in our life is being controlling, if we knew their backstory and the "why" of their behavior, we too might be more understanding. I'd wager that if we knew, we'd be more inclined to give them the benefit of the doubt and not assign wrong motives to their actions and behavior.

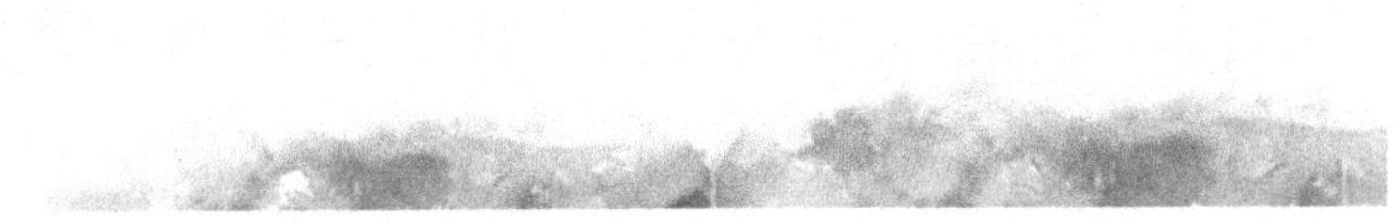

Chapter Ten: In Which We Go Deeper into the Woods and Discover a Different Ending

"Rivers know this: there is no hurry.
We shall get there some day."

A.A. Milne

Deeper into the Woods

This, like my previous book *Shameless: Set Free from the Mask*, is not a textbook. I am not a psychologist nor licensed therapist. I'm just a people-observing comic, who spent nearly 15 years serving in church and volunteer settings. I think I learned a thing or two about people. This book is written in the hopes that it will help you understand, accept and love yourself, so that you can understand, accept and love others. In my experience, there is no way that we can export that which we don't own or possess. Only when we can give ourselves grace and hold ourselves accountable for our own actions and behaviors can we extend the same courtesy toward others in a healthy way.

It would not surprise me if this book were to be of help or benefit to you in your work or business, but that's not its purpose. The purpose of this book is to help you in your relationships with those most important to you. Your spouse or partner, your children, your parents, your close friends... anyone of consequence in your life... starting with you.

Loneliness is an unnecessary and avoidable part of life. A common occurrence among the people that I've counseled over the years was that their loneliness was a choice. Weary and wounded, these dear people had given up on themselves and others, and they chose to withdraw in varying degrees. What they all had in common was that they did not understand themselves, so there was certainly no sense in even trying to understand someone else. This thinking led them to assume that they were somehow disqualified from ever having healthy relationships, because they were just "too screwed up," so they often chose loneliness over the fear of being rejected.

Humans are communal creatures and need to be in healthy relationships. Even people who say that they don't like people (and probably have good reasons for saying it) are in need of at least some level of community and relationship with others. History records the story of an ancient king, who was known for his great riches and wealth. He had many wives and concubines, yet near the end of his days he lamented that his life was devoid of friendships.

"I saw something the other day that was totally meaningless... it was a man who was working all alone. He didn't have any brothers or any sons. There seemed to be no end to his workday and yet he was not content with his vast wealth and accomplishments.

'Who am I working for?' the man asked himself, 'and why am I not enjoying the things I have accumulated? This miserable business of mine is meaningless!' I've come to understand that two people working together are better than one person working alone. The work is easier, gets done faster and they get a better return for their efforts. And if one of them were to fall ill or be injured the other one can help them. I feel sorry for anyone who's in need and there's no one around to help."

This king, a fellow named Solomon, is like so many people living today—he was lonely by choice. He ultimately chose wealth and riches over relationships, and I hope that after he wrote this lament that he changed his ways and didn't die a lonely death.

The Four A's

I'm a second-generation beneficiary of a program that helped my mother gain and retain sobriety until her passing in 1996. I am grateful to the organization,

Alcoholics Anonymous, who for decades has helped countless numbers of people discover a life of sobriety and are known affectionately by their initials, AA. In keeping with the spirit of helping people come to a self-awakening, keeping it simple and since they already used two A's, I'm going to use four A's.

The Four A's or "AAAA" is a practical way of helping those who have figured out their personality-type but are still struggling with loving themselves. By now if you've read each chapter and didn't skip around, shop online, or check football scores on your smart phone while you were reading, I purposely laid a foundation for what I'm about to share now.

In order to move toward loving ourselves, we don't have to like all the things we think, say or do. I've never met anyone who has completely pure thoughts or motives. I've never met anyone who has always done the right thing and I have never met anyone who has always said the right thing. If I'm not mistaken, the perfect person like that was crucified and died to cover all of our imperfections. No one is perfect. Preachers on TV? Not perfect. People who write books on marriage and relationships? Not perfect. How about people who write about personality-types? Not even remotely close to perfect. What we all have in common are our failures, flaws, foibles and fears. I've been in the entertainment industry for nearly 40 years, and you'd be surprised at the backstage conversations I've had with people who you think are flawless, but who hate their noses, ears, feet and things I can't mention without blushing. Sadly, money, fame, talent, beauty or success don't provide true happiness, because if they did then maybe, just maybe, we'd see less addiction and lower divorce rates than we do now.

What are the four A's? First and foremost, all four A's are verbs or "words of action" and are best defined (understood) and applied when putting the word "to" in front of them. They are:

To… acknowledge
To… accept
To… appreciate
To… adopt

Okay, so now what? It's not so much a "what" that's most important right now, but rather a "who?" But before we go there, let's dig a little deeper into the four A's.

To acknowledge doesn't mean a passing, detached or disgruntled, "Yeah, yeah I get it," attitude. To acknowledge means to know deeply to the point of admitting and conceding something as true and factual. That no matter what our feelings tell us about another person, an issue or even ourselves, we admit and concede that the facts are the facts. It's simple, but it's not easy, because feelings are always real, but they're not always correct. Most of us have a tendency to be harder on and less forgiving of ourselves than we are toward others. And yet we can also get quite defensive at times, too, can't we? Acknowledging that we are not perfect, that we are flawed and that we've made mistakes is just the start.

There is also the acknowledgment in that I recognize that I'm the only one of me that there is, and I'm the only one of me that I've got. I've done good things. I've made right choices and decisions. And even though I'm flawed, I'm in good company with the rest of humankind. I am capable of loving and worthy to receive love... um... that's a fact by the way. Like I said, it may be simple, but it's not easy.

To accept isn't a passive verb, it's more like taking hold of something... especially when accepting something that is valuable... like you. In some ways to accept means to welcome into. So, accepting some things that were completely beyond our control, like the shape of our ears, the family we were born to, our birth order or our personality is a good way to start. But that's just the start. Similar to acknowledgement, there are both good and bad things that were out of our control that require our acceptance. This isn't easy and can be extremely difficult for those who have suffered personal tragedy, trauma or any kind of abuse at the hands of another. No one, who has suffered in these ways, should try to travel the journey toward wholeness alone or without professional help. Been there, done that. *

There is also accepting responsibility for the things that were in our control. No one made us eat a second bowl of ice cream or the last doughnut. No one else packed that hotel towel in our suitcase or didn't tell the cashier they gave us too much change. We did that. It's kind of ironic now, isn't it? In some ways, we are harder on and less forgiving of ourselves; and yet in other things, we give ourselves a free pass and are harder on and much less forgiving when others hurt or wound us. You see, it's like a dog chasing its tail. We can laugh and laugh all we want from our vantage point, but from the dog's point of view, it makes perfect sense. We need to take hold of the fact that just as what we do is often beyond the control of others, what others have done (even to us) was often beyond our control. Are you paying attention, Rabbit, or have you decided to write me an angry email? It's okay if you do, I'll read it.

To appreciate is a very lovely verb. Appreciate... its four syllables just sound pleasant to the ear... appreciate. This word of action means to treasure, to admire or to behold with high regard. Have you ever considered treasuring yourself? To admire that you are an amazing mix of bone, muscle, neurotransmitters, synapses, tissues, ligaments and that the complexity of just your eyeball has kept scientists *wowed* for generations. Add to that, you are the original, the one and only you and the only you you've got. Sure, you've made some mistakes and there are some things that were and are out of your control and things that you can't change, but... you can change the way you look at and stiff arm yourself. Go ahead, admit it… you're a treasure that's been buried by your own sands of neglect.

To adopt is the "verbiest" (I know it's not a real word, Owl) of all the four A's. To adopt has a very special meaning to me because of five very special girls and two very special adults. In 2010 after the earthquake that shook Haiti to its core in 2009, a friend of mine, along with my then eighteen-year-old son and I went to Port au Prince for a few weeks. One day we visited a tent city orphanage and were overwhelmed at the number of children who had been without water for several days. Little did my friend, my son or I know that five years later, one of the little girls that we met that day along with her sister, two of her cousins and another little girl, who was not even related to her, would be living in the USA, as the legally adopted daughters of my friend and his wife. I love the word "adopt."

To adopt means to "take in as our very own" … not just our own… our very own. Adoption doesn't consider race, origin or creed. Adoption is a matter of the heart. It is a choice, when one person chooses another. There is emphasis, there is intent, and in its truest form, there is no ulterior motive, agenda and certainly no self-aggrandizing. It is solely based upon one's compassion and their desire to love, nurture and care for someone else. This includes (but not limited to their) physical, emotional, mental and spiritual needs. Sadly, many people have emotionally and mentally orphaned themselves. So, let's put some action to the four A's.

Masking

In my previous book, I wrote about the power and control that shame can have over our lives. Simply stated, shame is a shadowy force that has controlled people's thoughts, actions and lives for centuries. Without warning or fanfare, shame will appear and provoke us to run away, cover-up or hide our faces from things remembered from our past or an awkward, uncomfortable situation we are currently experiencing.

Shame is a mental health and relationship killer because at its core, shame is about keeping secrets and hiding from the truth. Read Genesis 3:6-11 for the first recorded "shame attack."

We've talked about the healthy and unhealthy versions of the four characters. When healthy, each of the four personalities will usually say or do kind things. The healthy version of our personality is not only welcome in relationships, but it also vital. We all benefit from the strengths that the four types offer to the mix.

That's why it's helpful to recognize and accept our weaknesses so we are not defensive or insecure when they are revealed. In addition, by recognizing and admitting our weaknesses we begin to appreciate and not feel threatened when others operate in their strengths.

Identifying and addressing our weaknesses is a whole lot harder than just putting on a mask. No one is proud of their flaws, foibles or mistakes. We want them to disappear and never come back, but they do and at some level they always will. It's how we deal with them that makes us a healthy Owl, Piglet, Rabbit or Tigger. When coming face to face with our weaknesses immediately turning away in embarrassment or shame is the first step in wearing a mask.

During the live presentation of *Who the Pooh are You? (WTPAY)*, while doing a fast overview of each character I can see the audience. Sometimes I think they forget that I can see them just as well as they can see me. While listing the traits of each character, individual audience members smile and nod in agreement as the characters are described and will choose the character that they think matches them and also the character that matches their spouse or people who came with them.

From my vantage point, It's fun to watch as audience members turn to one another and say things like, "That's so you!" or "Ohhh, that is so me!" Those smiles have a tendency to fade, and the nodding slows down when I start describing some of the weaknesses associated with each character.

It's funny how quickly they change their mind about which character they are. Suddenly, the character that they had originally identified with as being "their personality" is no longer their choice. Well... it was while listing the positive traits, but now... with all this new and uncomfortable information... that character is no longer their choice and they turn and say, "Never mind, that's not me at all, but that one is still you!" I watch this happen in real time every time I do this live. Why?

Maybe it's because we tend to be our own worst critic and when problematic areas of personality are identified or openly discussed, it hits too close to the bone, and we don't like what we see. I can't tell you how many times I've heard someone say after taking the WTPAY test that they don't want to be the personality that the results revealed. They don't deny or argue the results, they just don't like them. This goes back to the fundamental need for us to believe that we were created and intended to have this personality, we just have some work to do.

As a side note... people usually don't change their minds about which character they pegged their spouse or family member as, even as their character's particular problem areas are revealed. And why is that? Because it's not personal, that's why. When it's not personal we can be more judgey... I mean subjective.

What a mess

Using a house as a metaphor, if your house is a mess and you are expecting dinner guests, would you take a sheet and simply cover all your clutter in the foyer? Maybe shove your laundry in the oven? How about stuffing all your bills, papers and magazines under the couch cushions? The house "looks" great! But how will your guests get past the pile in the foyer? What are you going to serve now that the oven is otherwise occupied? Where is everyone going to sit? But hey... the house looks great! (And Tigger is satisfied with the cleverness).

It may "look" great, but it ain't great. It won't be long until you and your guests realize that it's actually quite awful and it's becoming awfully uncomfortable too. With sheets covering mounds of stuff, no food and nowhere to sit your guests are increasingly aware that all is not what it seems. It's the same when we try to mask the unaddressed or untended to weaknesses in our personalities.

Just for the sake of argument, let's say that you like your metaphorical house and that you have a healthy appreciation for it. When it is a mess, you know it. At the moment, you may be exhausted and don't have any desire or the strength to clean, but if you are a healthy person physically, mentally, emotionally and spiritually you will ultimately deal with the mess... this includes you too Tigger.

To properly deal with the mess, instead of being covered with a sheet, the clutter gets picked up, the laundry gets removed from the oven then it's washed, dried and put away, and after digging under the couch cushions, the bills get paid and the papers and magazines are filed, compiled or tossed. Now that's a great looking house. Every Owl reading this probably is experiencing a warm inner sensation right now.

It's much easier to cover, stuff and hide a mess than it is to deal with it. It takes less time and energy... at first anyway. Just like it takes work to actually clean your house, it takes work to maintain covering, stuffing and hiding the original mess as it continues to grow. It takes even more energy to cover up a mess than to clean it up because even though your messy house may appear clean, you cannot accept the truth that it really isn't. We can all try to convince ourselves that it's alright and we like it this way. And if you live a life of complete and total isolation, I guess you got me there. However, if you are reading this book, you are not the person I just described because you're reading a book about relationships.... So... I guess I got you.

Listen... I get it. My personality is not wired so that the moment I awake I'm excited to clean up the house or any other messes I've created or been party to. I know the temptation to sweep things under the rug until it becomes a mound. And it's for that very reason that I am now capable and motivated to clean rather than cover.

I've learned that covering just delays and eventually adds to my workload and efforts. Whether you are an Owl, Piglet, Rabbit or Tigger, avoiding the mess accomplishes very short-term gains which, in the long run, amounts to absolutely zero. And you've probably wasted a lot of mental and emotional energy on it and what has that benefited you? Again… absolutely zero.

Before proceeding, take a few moments to reflect on the messy house metaphor. What were your thoughts and feelings about the following aspects of the metaphor? Do any of these below come close to or align with your responses?

The messy house:
O - My house is never messy.
T - It doesn't bother me.
O - It drives me crazy.
R - Guests are coming, I have to do something.
T - It's not my job to clean house.
R - It's my house, it can stay a mess.
T - What mess?
O - None of those messes are mine.

The dinner guests:
O - This is why I fuss about keeping the house clean and tidy.
P - I have to hurry and clean.
T - They won't care.

T - I didn't know we were having dinner guests.
R - It's my house, I don't care what they think.

Covering, stuffing, hiding:
O - That makes my skin crawl.
P - I'd be so embarrassed.
T - That's a great idea.
R - Get out of my way, I'll do it.
P - Is this a good idea?
O - I hate when this happens.
T - No big, I've been doing this since college.

Addressing, cleaning, organizing:
O - It should have never gotten to this point.
P - Absolutely, I'll help.
R - You need to start with the laundry, here I'll do it.
T - Okay, I'll go to the store and get some ice cream.
R - It looks fine, it's not a big deal.
R - Why are we having people over in the first place?

Considering our four characters, Owl (O), Piglet (P), Rabbit (R) and Tigger (T), go back and write the first letter of each character next to the phrase you think would most describe their response.

Go back and write your first initial and the initials of your spouse, partner, parent, sibling with whom you share a house.
Each of the four characters typically have an initial thought or reaction to the scenario above and

sometimes it comes to fruition in their response and behavior. However, sometimes you'll be surprised by a less than predictable response.

Though each character usually has a "go to" or default setting in situations they also have the opportunity and ability to make a different choice than the one they typically choose.

Depending upon your mental or emotional state, it will either ignite your default setting or give you pause to consider if there is a better option. You might even discover after considering your options that your default setting is exactly what is needed in the moment.

Connecting to the Source: Winning in Weakness

"But He said to me, 'My grace is sufficient for you, for My power is made perfect in weakness.' Therefore, I will boast all the more gladly about my weaknesses, so that Christ's power may rest on me. That is why for Christ's sake, I delight in weaknesses, in insults, in hardships, in persecutions, in difficulties. For when I am weak, then I am strong." 2 Corinthians 12:9-11

Christians often quote the scripture above, or at least part of it. Most often a truncated version, "When I'm weak He is strong!" But there is context to consider and remember.

Think about the strengths of the four characters and what their personality offers to the other characters. Now consider the list of things that Paul "delights in" and how each character might not be so delighted.

Weakness? I'm pretty sure that's not something that Rabbit wants to admit while leading the team or a project. The word weakness is also translated as "infirmities" which the Bible uses for feeble, frailty or personal failings. No self-respecting Rabbit wants to be viewed as any of those "f" words.

Insults? Tigger just hates to be insulted, mocked or criticized at social gatherings. The word insults is also translated as "reproaches" which means to express disapproval or disappointment and what does Tigger seek... that's right, approval/acceptance.

Hardships? While working hard at providing care for others, Piglet certainly enjoys some additional troubles just to make things even harder. Hardship in scripture is often used to describe being overwhelmed by necessities in life. Piglet will be tempted to give out of their own lack which never ends well.

Persecutions? Owl with that innate sense of justice and following the rules is surely overcome with joy at being unfairly judged or persecuted for doing the right thing... right? Persecution often employs slander in its arsenal when damaging a person's reputation, and because, by definition, slander means "false" which just cuts an Owl even deeper.

Difficulties? This one is felt equally among the four characters as each character has their own list of what they deem difficult, and they will have several in common.

None of the characters are big fans of the five things that Paul "delights in," but they have a different weight or measure depending on your personality.

Rabbits have a hard time asking for help and will overcome by sheer determination and effort and really could care less if you insult them.

Tiggers can give a good jab and rarely takes one as well as they dispense them but have no problem asking for someone else to help them.

Piglets will interpret the hardship as yet one more reason it's all their fault and while they're at it, why not add some weakness or an insult to the mix.

Owl internalizes that it's not fair to be blamed, because they played by the rules while everyone else broke them. They are not a big fan of insults either, but hardships are just another opportunity to find solutions.

Gondola Stop #10

We've arrived at the end of our journey. *But I wanted a final word before we let you go.* And that word is simple and easy to remember. It's a word that has staying power. In fact, I believe that this word overcomes all our biggest handicaps.

I have some proof, so before I tell you the word, let me tell you a little story. It just happened two days ago, actually. I had been reading a book, *as I do*. And it caused me to ask my family a question. Here it is*: how is God using your weaknesses?*

Now I have one child, who answered quickly, "Memorizing scripture, because I actually remember it. And you know how I'm often forgetful? Not with scripture!" Another child answered, "You know how I have dyslexia? Well, I don't have any trouble reading my Bible. No trouble, at all."

So, my "word" for you is this: **Make the Word of God a daily part of your life.**

That is the gift I'm handing to you before we part ways, *until we meet again in the Bigger Story.*

Pick up your Bible, then read and memorize the Word of God. In fact, study it, like it matters. ('*Cause it does*!) Pray, as you go. Ask God to equip you for your part that He has prepared in advance for you to do. Ask God to soften the hard edges, to make you healthy, to give you a sound mind, to give you help in your weaknesses.

And He will do it. For from Him and through Him and to Him are all things. (Romans 11:36)

It is a way to distinguish yourself, to be set apart as His very own. It is also a way to celebrate the differences of others—to acknowledge your need of them to come with you in carrying out your calling. And when you do that, life is filled with God's glorious, marvelous, wonderful way over every BIG and little thing you see and hear and do.

*"Study to show yourself approved unto God, a workman who need not to be ashamed, rightly dividing the word of truth" (*1 Timothy 2:15 MEV).

And we will see you there! Cannot wait to hear all the stories...they're gonna be so good!

Bibliography: In Which We Cite Notable Citations

Introduction

Quote (Source https://www.goodreads.com/quotes/5099965-the-things-that-make-me-different-are-the-things-that)

Citation (Source the Holy Bible Ephesians 2:10 Paul)

Chapter One

*Citation (Source: Oxford dictionary)

Chapter Two

Quote (Source: https://www.goodreads.com/quotes/142015-when-you-are-a-bear-of-very-little-brain-and or https://en.wikiquote.org/wiki/A. A. Milne)

*Citation (Source : www.nytimes.com "Chances are you're Codependent Too" by Wendy Kraminer Published 2/11/1990)

**Citation (Source: the Holy Bible Proverbs 22:6 King Solomon)

*** Citation (Source: The Five Love Languages by Dr. Gary Chapman Moody Press)

Codependency is a dysfunctional – and common – relationship model. Its origin is usually linked to childhood. Children who are raised to believe that their feelings aren't significant learn to live through other people's emotions, leading to codependent behavior. The prevalence of codependency is difficult to ascertain. Some estimates suggest that over 90 percent of the American population demonstrates codependent behavior. A study by Crester and Lombardo (1999) found that nearly half of surveyed college students displayed middle or high codependent characteristics.

Chapter Three

Quote (Source: https://www.goodreads.com/quotes/28088-the-third-rate-mind-is-only-happy-when-it-is-thinking)
Citation (Source: The Holy Bible John 11:6, John 14:4-6, John 20:24-28)

Chapter Four

*Recommended reading: Boundaries "When to Say Yes, How to Say No to Take Control of Your Life" by Henry Cloud and John Townsend/Zondervan Publishing
** Citation (Source: The Holy Bible Proverbs 22:6, paraphrase)
Source (The Holy Bible Ruth)
Quote (Source: https://www.goodreads.com/quotes/125307-i-m-not-lost-for-i-know-where-i-am-but)

Chapter Five

Quote (Source: https://www.goodreads.com/quotes/46807-organization-is-what-you-do-before-you-do-something-so)

Citation (Source: Paraphrase from The Holy Bible Exodus 2-40, Leviticus, Numbers, Matthew 17:2-4)

Chapter Six

Citation (Source: The Holy Bible Judges 13:1-16:30; Hebrews 11:32)
Quote (https://www.goodreads.com/quotes/140865-oh-tigger-where-are-your-manners-i-don-t-know-but)

Chapter Seven

Quote (Source: https://www.goodreads.com/quotes/223700-what-day-is-it-asked-pooh-it-s-today-squeaked-piglet)

Citation (Source: The Holy Bible Romans 11:29, 2 Peter 1:3, 1 Corinthians 14:26-33)

Chapter Eight

Quote (Source: https://www.goodreads.com/quotes/41130-you-can-t-stay-in-your-corner-of-the-forest-waiting)

Chapter Nine

Quote (Source: https://www.goodreads.com/quotes/19370-if-the-person-you-are-talking-to-doesn-t-appear-to)

Citation* (Source: The Five Love Languages by Dr. Gary Chapman)

Citation (Source: The Holy Bible Proverbs 22:6)

Chapter Ten

Quote (Source: https://www.goodreads.com/quotes/210608-rivers-know-this-there-is-no-hurry-we-shall-get)

Citation (Source: The Holy Bible 2 Corinthians 12:9-11, 1 Timothy 2:15)

In Which We Share Other Works by the Authors

Steve Geyer, *Shameless: Set Free from the Mask* (Winnipeg, MB: Word Alive Press 2016).

Alisa Hope Wagner, Holly Smith, et al., *Granola Bar Devotionals: Spiritual Snacks on the Go!* (Corpus Christi, TX, Marked Writers Publishing 2018)

Alisa Hope Wagner, Holly Smith, et al., *Get to the Margins: A Devotional Anthology of Writers on the Edge* (Corpus Christi, TX, Marked Writers Publishing 2018)

Alisa Hope Wagner, Holly Smith, et al., *Kissing Guilt Goodbye: Breaking Free from the Shackles of Shame* (Corpus Christi, TX, Marked Writers Publishing 2020)

Alisa Hope Wagner, Holly Smith, et al., *Pandemic Devotionals: How the World Overcame Fear with Faith* (Corpus Christi, TX, Marked Writers Publishing 2021)

Appendix A

Who the Pooh are You?

Place a number between 1 & 4 (4 being the most like you & 1 being the least like you) beside each descriptive word(s) below. When you are finished, add up the points for each section and place them in the appropriate space.

4 = most like you
3 = moderately like you
2 = moderately not like you
1 = not like you at all

_____ Mathematical
_____ Analytical
_____ Perfectionist
_____ Methodical
_____ Judgmental
_____ Exacting (everything in its place)
_____ Detailed
_____ Realist
_____ Major decisions - "think it over"
_____ Conscientious
_____ Checking account balanced to the penny
_____ System oriented
_____ Non-risk taker
_____ Usually on time
_____ Neat-neat
_____ Slow paced
_____ Prefers security to prestige
_____ Doesn't like over excitement
_____ Clothes are hung up at night
_____ Enjoys being alone

_____ TOTAL POINTS FOR "O"

Hard driving _____
Commanding _____
Fearless _____
Cynical _____
Opinionated _____
Courageous _____
Authoritative _____
Prefers others to "Pick-up" for them _____
Prestige more important than security _____
Bold _____
Competitive _____
Decisive _____
Venturesome _____
Organizer _____
Likes people to get to the point _____
Bottom-line is important _____
Organized-messy person _____
Fast to decide _____
Love a challenge _____
Usually "always" right _____

TOTAL POINTS FOR "R" _____

_____ Amiable
_____ Passive
_____ Unhurried
_____ Sensitive
_____ Kind
_____ Cooperative
_____ Warm
_____ Patient
_____ Mild
_____ Steady
_____ Dependable
_____ Non-judgmental
_____ Non-risk taker
_____ Usually on time for fear of others' opinions
_____ Indecisive
_____ Avoids Conflict
_____ Slow to make decisions
_____ Frequently changes mind
_____ Prefers other's opinions
_____ Security is more important than prestige

_____ TOTAL POINTS FOR "P"

Expressive _____
Impulsive _____
Talkative _____
Promoter _____
Dreamer _____
Very socially oriented _____
Hospitable _____
Trusting _____
Eager _____
Fun Loving _____
Optimistic _____
Enthusiastic _____
Risk Taker _____
Often late _____
Messy _____
Leaves clothes where taken off _____
Likes excitement _____
Social relationships very important _____
Recognition is important _____
Non-detailed (prefers others to do it) _____

TOTAL POINTS FOR "T" _____

For a randomized *Who the Pooh are You?* Assessment or the one on the page before, please follow the link below:

https://hishollysmith.org/who-the-pooh-are-you-quiz/

Also, you can print out any of them, as well!

Appendix B

Excellent resources available on discovering your personality-type:

The Five Love Languages by Dr. Gary Chapman

Personality Plus by Florence Littauer

Mere Christianity by C.S. Lewis

Made in USA - Kendallville, IN
68526_9781486620234
02.05.2024 2209